Written Communications for MIS/DP Professionals

The Macmillan Database/Data Communications Series

Shaku Atre, Consulting Editor

Written Communications for MIS/DP Professionals

Larry M. Singer
Ross Laboratories
A Division of Abbott Laboratories

MACMILLAN PUBLISHING COMPANY
NEW YORK

Collier Macmillan Publishers
LONDON

Macmillan Publishing Company
866 Third Avenue, New York, NY 10022

Collier Macmillan Canada, Inc.

Printed in the United States of America

printing number
1   2   3   4   5   6   7   8   9   10

Library of Congress Cataloging in Publication Data

Singer, Larry M. (Larry Martin), 1946–
    Written communications for MIS/DP professionals.

    (Macmillan database/data communications series)
    Includes index.
    1. Management information systems.   2. Communication in
management.   I. Title.   II. Title: Written communications
for M.I.S./D.P. professionals.   III. Series.
T58.6.S563   1985   658.4'038   85-10494
ISBN 0-02-947870-7

Contents

v

Preface

Data processing today is critical to the very existence of many companies, from the local hardware store to the largest multinational conglomerate. Yet many organizations that have their own MIS departments, or who work through service bureaus and other professional service companies, are disappointed with general MIS performance. There are delays in developing new systems, misunderstandings between users and the technical staff, and embarrassing confusion among the MIS employees themselves. Computers may be powerful machines capable of amazing feats of computation, but the people in charge of MIS seem to be unable to put everything together. Why?

One reason is *poor written communication*. Many data-processing managers and technicians simply cannot effectively pass on information through the written word, and the ultimate cost to the organization is staggering. Productivity suffers, morale declines, and user confidence drops.

This book helps provide the solution. Each chapter is a self-contained unit that addresses a critical need in the MIS department. Many chapters have sample formats—from business plans that make sense to memos that actually communicate.

Even more important, this book presents working MIS documents that are a direct extension of a sound management philosophy. Every document in MIS should be carefully engineered to follow management direction! *Good technical writing encourages good management.*

This book is for everyone in MIS who deals with the written word. Many of the answers are here!

Larry M. Singer

Acknowledgments

I wish to thank the many people in my professional life who taught me the value of good written communication.

I also thank my wife, Carolyn, who helped prepare the manuscript, and my son, Shane, who for several long months graciously shared his father with That Word Processor in the Living Room.

L.M.S.

Written Communications for MIS/DP Professionals

chapter *1*

Written Communication in MIS

INTRODUCTION

This chapter defines written technical and business communication, describes the value of written communication, and lists some of the documents used in the typical MIS department. It emphasizes that written communication not only is an extension of management policy, but in effect *becomes* management policy! This chapter also evaluates the growing importance of technical writing in terms of today's rapidly changing technology. All directors, managers, supervisors, systems analysts, technical writers, programmers, and users should understand the importance and the role of communication in the MIS organization.

Written technical and business documentation includes any paper (or online text system) used to convey information about an MIS activity. This includes such widely varying documents as project proposals, memos, project plans, status reports, transcripts, business plans, budgets, system designs, programming specifications, feasibility studies, operating instructions, and user manuals. Virtually every form of person-to-person communication, except perhaps oral statements and body language, falls within the scope of written communication. And virtually everyone in the MIS organization uses, writes, or updates technical documents. Further, many people in other departments rely heavily on the written communication of MIS employees.

This book should be read by anyone who creates, reads, or approves the following documents:

- Proposals
- Feasibility statements
- Business plans
- Requirements documents
- System designs
- Cost-benefits analyses
- Programming specifications
- Chronological history files
- Service requests
- Project status reports
- Task control forms
- Weekly status reports
- Experience evaluation forms
- Monthly and quarterly reports
- Memos

- User manuals
- Operational run sheets
- Problem-reporting logs
- Special procedures documentation
- Master system documentation
- Data-center statistics reports
- Vendor evaluation forms
- Reference letters for software purchases
- Software comparison charts
- Program-level documentation
- Flow charts
- System "answer books"
- System logs

1.1 THE IMPORTANCE OF WRITTEN COMMUNICATION

Many experienced data-processing professionals and managers fail to appreciate the critical nature of the entire written communication process. Subjectively, MIS as a whole is often judged by the quality of various written documents. People tend to think that a confused, illogical, and hard-to-understand memo comes from a confused, illogical, and hard-to-understand person! Written material represents not only the author, but the entire department as well. Objectively, as MIS departments become larger and more involved with the day-to-day operation of their organizations, their written output becomes more important. Therefore, the value of all forms of communication is increasing. No longer are MIS employees dealing with small, easily controlled projects or application systems; today some MIS projects involve millions of dollars and massive company commitments. Government regulatory agencies often review internal and external MIS documentation before certifying computerized systems. MIS is always a highly visible part of most organizations—witness the outcry when an online system fails in the middle of the day!

But things are not always perfect in the world of MIS. Company executives complain of consistently late projects, poor-quality application systems, and a user-MIS relationship that resembles a war zone. The classic excuse is "We didn't know." Users say they cannot understand MIS professionals. Programmers and analysts complain they cannot understand users. Programmers often say they cannot understand analysts. Computer operators have trouble understanding programmers. MIS directors are puzzled by their inability to control events. MIS employees as a group are frustrated by the "management-by-crisis" atmosphere that seems to pervade many data-processing environments. And everyone is upset by the surprises, misunderstandings, mistakes, and confusion that surround even many routine MIS activities like a hovering cloud.

What separates the smoothly running MIS departments from the ones that wander from one crisis to the next? Why are some departments functioning like efficient information factories that produce exactly what they say when they say it? Why do others resemble a collection of fragmented individuals who have trouble communicating with the person in the next office?

Obviously, there is no single answer that applies to all

situations. But one basic, underlying factor that helps distinguish the efficient from the nonefficient (or the "professional" from the "nonprofessional") is the quality of written technical communication. The difference is not necessarily in quantity but rather in *quality*. Well-managed departments tend to use clear, concise, and accurate means of communication. Their employees know when to pick up a phone and when to reach for a word processor. They know how much to write and how to communicate the essential ideas to readers. They deliberately make the entire communication process easier for themselves and their users. Such employees understand how efficient communication improves productivity.

1.2 MANAGEMENT POLICY AND TECHNICAL WRITING

Managers assume that documents, memos, and forms will automatically support their decisions, orders, and direction. This assumption is often false—nothing of the sort "automatically" occurs! In theory, paperwork should always be consistent with official policy, but many managers do not realize that because of the *intrinsic power* of documents, written communications *become* management direction. The MIS director and staff can order any policy they want, but if the documents that run the department and its activities do not help implement that policy, the directive is lost.

For example, if an MIS manager demands improved project status information but the department continues to use an old form not suited to that directive, that request has been effectively ignored. If the MIS director wants to ensure the feasibility of potential projects before authorizing development funds, the director's orders are worthless unless the systems analysts begin using efficient feasibility statements. Employees need the proper tools to carry out their manager's orders. Every document in data processing should support management's general direction and specific policies; if this is not done, over the long term the department will generally follow the direction *perceived* from the written documentation. In many cases, forms and documents have no obvious direction, since they were created in piecemeal fashion, and confusion wins by default! Written documents and their accompanying procedures often set the tone for the entire department! MIS directors can strive for better communication within their own groups and with their user communities, but unless they improve the forms, procedures, and reports used in daily activities, they may be wasting their time.

1.3 HOW DOES TECHNOLOGY AFFECT TECHNICAL WRITING?

The explosive growth of distributed data processing has increased the already dramatic need for good written communication. As computer power becomes more available to smaller companies and many departments become physically separated from MIS, users rely more on written documentation. It is in fact their key to survival. Whereas the "help desk" concept is important, users still require visual instructions to maintain their hardware and software environments.

The use of low-cost microcomputers has opened vast markets for good software that comes with clear, easy-to-follow documentation. Time-sharing services require explicit online help functions that allow users to understand their services. Interfacing various application systems requires absolutely correct and understandable information. Some companies now screen potential software packages by evaluating their written documentation! The trend toward online processing has not diminished the value of documentation; instead, it has created a new set of requirements for "intelligent" documentation on a CRT.

1.4 THE LAWS OF MIS DOCUMENTATION

Unfortunately for the business world, only professional technical writers seem to prepare themselves for the process of written communication. Everyone else seems to trust their skills to fate. As in a Greek tragedy, fate is not always kind, but by observing some MIS departments in action, one can often predict when and why things go wrong!

The problems associated with poor written communication can even be described in mathematical terms:

1. The number of problems in a new computer system is inversely proportional to the quality of the written specifications.

2. The older the documentation, the more likely it is to be wrong.

3. The more the documentation reads like a poorly written COBOL program, the higher the likelihood that only a poor COBOL programmer can understand it.

4. The greater the number of undocumented changes to a system, the higher the probability that those changes will be wrong, or that no one will understand the changes even if they are correct.

5. The more a company relies on meetings and discussions to settle issues without documenting the results, the more misunderstandings will occur.

6. The greater the number of misunderstandings, the greater the probability that one of them will destroy the basic usefulness of the entire project.

7. The number of serious design flaws in any computer system is directly proportional to the number of times the designers say, "No, we don't need to write that down."

1.5 CONCLUSION

There are now few excuses for tolerating ambiguities, confusion, and potential misunderstandings in MIS person-to-person communication. Other professions learned long ago that precise written documentation was essential to their survival. Architects, for example, generally design bridges with detailed blueprints before the building process begins, and the output tends to be correct—the two ends of a bridge meet exactly in the center. Tunnels blasted through mountains seem to always meet in the center. But the relatively young profession of data processing has not learned that success is partially based on clearly written facts on paper.

Improving written communication is no longer a low-priority issue. MIS directors have too many critical responsibilities to ignore the problem, and there is no longer any justification for trusting written communication skills to the fates. Technical and business writing is merely a skill that one can and should improve without feeling personal embarrassment. Now that management development books, seminars, and courses have been widely accepted, perhaps MIS professionals and managers can admit that since programmers need to learn programming and managers need to learn managing, most MIS employees also need to develop effective written communication skills.

This book is for those who are ready to learn.

chapter **2**

Effective Writing: A Short Course

INTRODUCTION

This chapter explains the basics of effective writing: learning the objective attitude, using logical statements that match the purpose of the document, analyzing the audience, and defining key terms and phrases. It tells you how to add a positive style to your work using the natural approach. Finally, it describes specific ways to review your own work and locate those areas that need improvement. This is a short technical guide for those who would like to improve their own writing skills. The summary lists two books that will provide additional information on good writing techniques.

MIS professionals communicate by such varied means as system proposals, memos, user manuals, internal program documentation forms, customer request forms, operational instructions, and status reports of every conceivable description. The formats and purposes of the documents may differ, but the principles behind any piece of good writing remain the same. Effective written communication in any occupation or business follows several quite logical and relatively simple techniques.

Many people never try learning the skills of effective written communication, although some lucky individuals seem to be born with a natural ability. Those without this rare gift may never attempt to improve their written skills because they feel defensive or are actually ashamed of their writing performance. This attitude is common but counterproductive. Writing is merely another skill to be learned, just as one learns to analyze a system, locate a program error, manage a department, or even pluck a chicken. Indeed, the best analogy is to compare the task of writing to the practice of chicken plucking. Give anyone a chicken and they can eventually pluck most of the feathers; give anyone a pen, a typewriter, or a word processor and they will eventually write something. But in the real world there is a significant difference between a chicken well-plucked in a cost-effective manner and a chicken half-plucked after three hours of frustrating effort. In the second instance the company with too many costly but improperly plucked chickens may be on the road to bankruptcy. Unfortunately for most data-processing installations, far too many documentation projects resemble half-plucked chickens.

Writing skills can be learned, even by those who were not born with a natural writing ability. All it takes is a little common sense, a few basic guidelines, and a willingness to practice. Most important, however, is the ability to constructively criticize your own work. Unless you are taking a writing course or have a very willing tutor, it is unreasonable to expect others to spend their valuable time analyzing your written communication in detail and making line-by-line or word-by-word suggestions. In most situations, MIS professionals or managers are on their own. The right attitude is: I will be my own critic. The correct expectation is: Criticizing my own work may be painful, but the results will be worth it.

2.1 PLAN BEFORE YOU WRITE: LOGIC, AUDIENCE, TERMINOLOGY

Step 1: Match the purpose with logic. Before one picks up a pen or starts keying into a terminal, the first step is to analyze the purpose of the document. If the author is not clear about the ultimate goal and the ideas that need to be expressed, the best writing techniques in the world will not save the document.

Planning before writing helps make the document *logical.* Every piece of writing (or every piece that is actually understood by its readers) is partially judged by its degree of logic—only those memos, reports, and proposals that demonstrate logical thinking will stand out in the mind of the reader. But what is logical communication?

Illogical writing is actually easier to define, because it stands out like a payroll check $30,000 too high! People notice it immediately. But unlike the payroll error, which is an object of laughter, the illogical document is ignored, rejected, or scorned. The author too may be ignored, rejected, or scorned, even if the idea is basically sound. It may not be fair, but many people in this world ascribe to the author the same characteristics they give to the written communication! Many excellent ideas in MIS (and in other professions) never get off the ground because the author did not present them logically. Every phrase and sentence in the document must appear to be logical.

Consider the case of two bicycle repairmen from Dayton, Ohio, who wrote a proposal to their local bank in the early 1900s for funds to develop a new device called an "areoplane":

> Wilbur and I think that man can fly. If birds can, why can't people? This has been our dream since we were boys.

Other inventors are now working on flying machines, and we can do it, too.

The second sentence, which compares birds to men, is illogical, because the author provides no further support for his contention. Emotionally, the sentence could be appealing, but it is totally unsuited for a business proposal. Logical writing often equates with appropriateness. The banker may stop at this point and reject all following arguments, because people sometimes unconsciously assume that if one statement is illogical, so is the entire idea. The third statement, that other inventors are developing flying machines, is indeed worthy of further discussion, for it suggests a potential business venture. But the previous sentence ruins the proposal. Birds are very light and have wings, whereas people are heavy and don't have wings. Any fool knows that! No wonder people cannot fly! Why don't those brothers stick to repairing bicycles and forget the whole silly idea?

Step 2: Analyze the audience. If the ideas (and supporting reasons) are logical, the next step is to define the audience in terms that will help the author shape the document for the audience's specific needs. If it is an individualized memo, the reader is obvious, but for many pieces of professional documentation the audience may be several people with varying backgrounds and varying degrees of interest in the subject. In practice, the vast majority of written communication is given to multiple readers instead of a single individual, and authors should consider the "group" as their audience. This makes it even more essential to consider the audience before writing.

The following passage is from an operations manual designed to inform data entry operators of the procedures for requesting personal time away from the job:

Operators must fill out a PRS-42 with approval from an E-7 or above in that unit and give the required advance notice, as specified in the current version of Corporate Personnel Manual number 4 for nonexempt employees.

Such wording is obviously inappropriate for data entry operators who have never seen Corporate Personnel Manual number 4 and may not know an E-7 from a Z-2. A more effective description would be:

> If you need time off during the day, get a PRS-42 from the department secretary. Check the "personal" box, answer questions 1 through 4, and have either your supervisor or the unit manager sign the form. Send the form to Personnel at least three working days before the scheduled absence.

Although the second version contains more words, any data entry operator reading the document would immediately understand the procedure. There is no room for misunderstanding, because the author has considered the interests and experience level of the audience.

Any writer must also remember the limitations of the readers. Will the board of directors understand the advantages of a data-base approach to the new online order entry system? Should the proposal explain the critical differences between data-base and conventional file designs? Do the directors care? Or would they be more concerned with the long-term cost issues involved? Do they even understand the exact meaning of "data base" in this project? Will computer operators automatically understand the business purpose behind the credit processing system and the legal implications involved in production delays? Do they really need to know? If the answer is yes, the document written for computer operators must include those facts but avoid using terms that are more appropriate for the legal department.

At the same time, the writer must avoid insulting the intelligence of the reader. After all, knowledge about a given subject (or lack of knowledge) does not always equate with a person's innate intelligence. Albert Einstein may not have known much about his car, but a mechanic would have made a serious mistake in telling the white-haired old gentleman, "Don't worry, Al. It's very complicated. I don't think you could understand. Just trust me."

Consider the following set of instructions written for data entry operators:

Take off your coat. Hang it in the closet. Sit down at your station. Lock your purse in the top right-hand drawer. Start work when the clock says 8:30. Look at the top left-hand corner of the screen. If nothing appears, turn the intensity knob toward the right. If nothing appears then, raise your hand and ask for help.

Most experienced data entry operators would laugh at such childish and obviously insulting instructions. Laughing at a document may be a bad response, but it is preferable to another human emotion caused by underestimating the vice president of sales. Consider the following proposal:

Computers can only add, subtract, multiply, and divide, but they can help you track sales activity. Measuring the sales effort is hard. As a vice president, you want to know who has sold how much product and who has sold the least. Isn't that important? You also want to know the relative gross margin of each sale. Isn't that also important?

As a general rule, unless you are a senior vice president, president, chairperson of the board, major stockholder, valued customer, or highly paid consultant, you seldom *tell* vice presidents anything. In fact, you seldom *tell* anyone anything. Your personal attitude will usually surface in written communication, and even if you have sized your readers correctly in terms of their sophistication and interest, you must always treat them with respect. After all, if the readers are not worth a little respect, why bother writing to them at all?

Step 3: Define the terms and expressions. Whatever the first ten commandments are, the eleventh commandment in technical writing should be to "define thy terms." A very common complaint heard from readers of MIS documents is that they do not understand the vocabulary or buzzwords. Is it only the reader's responsibility to investigate every word? Definitely not! Much of the responsibility lies directly with the author.

Names and terms in data processing can have virtually opposite meanings to different people, depending on their experience, background, education, job responsibility, and mood when reading the document. If one asked ten different systems analysts to define the commonly heard phrase, "acceptable online response time," one would get at least fifteen answers. If one asked the same question a week later, one might hear a new set of sixteen answers. The final definition selected by the MIS manager may change when he or she discovers the cost difference between providing one-second or three-second response times. Readers do not have to accept the definitions in a document, but they must understand the author's original definition. Communication is difficult unless the author and the readers have a common basis for understanding.

The confusion over technical terms is even more pronounced when communicating with other professions. Business procedures such as LIFO and FIFO may sound like two French poodles to a programmer/analyst, whereas a common MIS phrase such as "local area network" could mean the television station down the street to an accountant. Imagine the misunderstanding when the programmer/analyst and the accountant are trying to design an inventory valuation system on a proposed collection of microcomputers linked together using a broadband communication network. The MIS professional isn't any smarter than the accountant; both have their areas of expertise, but both have a professional responsibility to provide clear, adequate, and useful definitions for any topic or word that could be misinterpreted.

Murphy's law also applies to written communication: if any term *can* be misunderstood, it *will* be.

When the audience is not in MIS, successful technical writers sometimes choose the words that are more meaningful to the readers rather than the words they prefer themselves. Every author has a vast array of word choices when creating a document, and the ultimate choice should be partially influenced by the mind-set of the reader. What words does the reader want to hear? Efficient written communication is concerned with the reader's expectation just as much as with the writer's knowledge.

2.2 THE NATURAL APPROACH TO STYLE

Style is just as important in technical writing as it is in the rest of life. Data-processing people do not like to read a poorly written COBOL program any more than they like to read a poorly written memo, system proposal, or user manual. Nontechnical readers dislike confusing written material even more! Like beauty, however, style is truly in the eye of the beholder, and one can find many ways to achieve a good writing style. This chapter will suggest the *natural* approach, which is relatively easy for both beginning and experienced writers to understand.

Writing with *style* often means that the document seems natural. Problems occur when writers attempt to become something they are not. As a general rule, the more complicated and formal the author tries to become, the worse the document. A natural piece of writing, on the other hand, has the correct blend of vocabulary, sentence structure, phrasing, and logical organization to help the reader feel comfortable. The reader may not agree with or even fully understand all the information, but the author has successfully communicated on a person-to-person level. The reader feels positive. New writers can learn this smooth blend of vocabulary, sentence structure, phrasing, and logical organization by consciously trying to become natural. There are five proven techniques that will help the author develop a natural style.

Use formal conversation as a model. This advice is often misunderstood, because it is often stated as "Write the way you talk." There are significant differences, however, between formal writing, formal conversation, and informal conversation. Consider the following memo from Peter Panic, Director of Operations, to Lana Ledger, Accounting Manager:

Pursuant to the timing agreement reached on June 2, 1985, please be aware that on at least four known occasions the Accounts Payable staff (APS) has requested an extension of the agreed-on deadline. Granting these requests to extend the standard APS hours for both inquiry and update has directly resulted in delays in the critical path, including a two-hour delay in starting the online order entry function, which resulted in an estimated dollars loss of Type II orders of not less than $10,000, nor more than $20,000.

Peter's memo reads like a legal summons, and Lana Ledger may wonder whether she should retain legal counsel before the matter reaches the Supreme Court! In reality, Peter is simply notifying Lana of a problem that needs resolution. The information in the document is accurate, but the style is unnatural. Formal writing is justified only on formal occasions, which occur very rarely in MIS, and Peter could have communicated the same information orally with an *informal conversation:*

Lana, we've been late in the critical path four times during the past two months. One time caused a delay in order processing, and Mark Muscle thinks we lost up to $20,000 in Type II orders! On those four occasions my people allowed APS to extend its operating hours. If you recall, back in June of 1984 we agreed on fairly strict APS hours. We want to help you guys out, but you see what can happen. I don't want that jerk Mark Muscle on my case again! You know how he can be. Can we talk about this problem?

The style of a phone call may be extremely natural (assuming Peter and Lana know each other well), but informal conversation is unsuited for written communication. If Peter insists on writing a memo, he should use the style of *formal conversation,* which in many cases helps create a very natural blend of vocabulary and sentence phrasing:

On four occasions during the past two months we have been late in the critical path. In fact, during one of those delays we could not bring up order entry for two hours and lost up to $20,000 in Type II orders. I have traced each of those occurrences to a request by APS to extend its online inquiry and update hours. Naturally, we try to accommodate APS, because we know how your workload piles up. But when Operations violates the schedule we agreed to back in June of 1985, we risk delaying the critical path and losing more orders. I suggest we discuss this problem as soon as possible.

The preceding example of formal conversation transferred to paper (or electronic mail) carries all the important information, suggests a cooperative spirit, and uses a natural style that makes the reader feel comfortable. *A natural writing style lets the reader concentrate on the material rather than the writing itself.*

Be honest with yourself and your readers. The old-fashioned virtue of honesty is important in every type of human communication. The most effective writing tends to come from authors who use their natural tendencies to *write as they believe.* One should seldom, if ever, distort facts or misrepresent the truth, because the quality of work will usually decrease. Only professional or experienced writers are capable of presenting information they do not accept themselves. Lawyers, for example, require intensive practice before they can disregard personal feelings and create legal briefs for an opinion they do not share. It can be done, but it requires special training. If at all possible, professionals in MIS should write what they consider the truth—only on rare occasions should they ignore this important rule.

Anticipate questions. Readers who are interested in the subject may have important questions as they read the document, and good technical writing provides the answers as the reader develops the questions! The most common question is: What happens if...? Unsophisticated users especially may wonder about matters that would shock the average MIS professional. Other readers may silently ask themselves questions but hesitate to appear stupid, even to themselves. What happens if the customer on the phone suddenly cancels the order? Must the order taker call data processing for help? Should the supervisor be called? Has the user ruined a $5-million computer? The answer to the question may be given in the appendix or on page 49, but the reader starts to worry on page 2!

Consumers of technical documents often need to know their responsibilities in detail when something goes *wrong*. Customers on the phone do cancel orders after saying, "Forget it. I'll call back. My three-year-old just got a headlock on the German shepherd." Data entry operators accidentally call up the weekly update screen instead of the online inquiry. Users get strange codes on their CRTs. The warehouse manager reading a proposal for a new location system wonders what will happen when the computer goes down. The author has a special responsibility to anticipate obvious questions and problems and to incorporate the answers directly in the text. In the world of data processing, people often care more about what happens when things go *wrong* than what happens when things go *right*.

Use examples. Even the most thorough explanations of a proposed idea, concept, or procedure can be confusing, because people rarely think in a formal, descriptive manner. Nontechnical readers reject documents that have the slightest hint of complexity, and many MIS professionals themselves dislike long verbal explanations. The best way to explain complicated matters is to provide examples and verbal illustrations. The examples can be serious, humorous, or somewhere in between, but readers have a better chance of understanding when the document provides concrete examples. People can relate better to an example than to a long, verbal narrative.

New technical writers and systems analysts occasionally forget there are situations in which humorous examples are inappropriate. When writing to a senior MIS manager about the need for training, one would not create a funny story about a clumsy MIS director who could not even turn on a CRT. Humor is justified only when the story or example does not attack others who may either read the document or hear about the humorous example. Humor does help communication, but consideration for others is always more important.

As a general rule, the more complicated the information, the more one needs examples. Furthermore, when the material is extremely dry, the author should consider including an occasional example merely to liven up the document. Murphy made another observation related to boring technical writing: If the reader can fall asleep, he or she *will*.

Vary the sentence structure.   Any document with a consistent, repetitive sentence structure is unbelievably depressing to both mind and body and always seems unnatural. Consider the following subtle example:

> The purpose of the inventory control system (ICS) is to control inventory and reduce investment. ICS tells the buyers how much they have and how much it costs. It also helps track purchase orders and discovers overstock situations. The buyers need ICS and ICS needs the buyers. They must pay close attention to the reports and they must correct errors as soon they appear. ICS interfaces with the sales system and it also interfaces with the accounting system. Management uses the summary ICS reports and the buyers use the detailed ICS reports.

After several more paragraphs the reader would fall into a singsong mental pattern, because each sentence contains two thoughts with the conjunction "and." Most readers would anticipate the next sentence! After simply rearranging the sentence structure, the paragraph conveys the same information without causing terminal boredom for anyone doomed to study the ICS system documentation.

> The purpose of the inventory control system (ICS) is to control inventory and reduce the inventory investment. Because it tracks purchase orders and discovers overstock situations, ICS tells the buyers how much they have and its relative cost. ICS also interfaces with both the accounting system and the sales system, which requires ICS errors to be corrected immediately. In general, management looks at the summary ICS reports and the buyers

use the detailed ICS output. ICS is an important tool for many departments here at Wonderful Widgets.

Deliberately varying the sentence structure should not be carried to extremes, because the document will look as if it had been generated by a computer rather than a human. Using a small assortment of phrases, conjunctions, and clauses will make the document appear natural.

2.3 REVIEWING YOUR WORK FOR CONCISENESS AND CLARITY

Writing is an art as well as a skill, and one can perfect an art form only by practice. But technical writers (including programmers, analysts, and managers) seldom get the feedback that artists need to polish their craft. Instead, authors in MIS and other professions must be their own critics, and the only realistic method is to review their own work. After the words are typed or printed from the word processor, the authors must change their mental set from that of creator to that of critic. The authors must now play the role of an interested reader who is not afraid to suggest changes or improvements. Once technical writers have accepted the fact that their creations are not perfect, they can begin the laborious process of improving their communication.

Technical writing has often been criticized for its wordiness, and the solution is to make every sentence concise and clear. A concise sentence or phrase comes directly to the point, without going around the proverbial mulberry bush, through the proverbial mulberry bush, or on top of the proverbial mulberry bush. Consider the following example:

> The accounting department will consider all important variables and work in conjunction with Data Entry to develop a mutually agreed-on schedule in terms of month-end cutoffs as they affect both Accounting and Data Entry.

The statement should be more direct:

The accounting department will work with the data entry department to develop a mutually satisfactory month-end cutoff schedule.

The two sentences convey essentially the same message, but the second uses less than half the words. Although word counts are not always a valid measure of conciseness, the first example is so long the reader may get lost in the mulberry bush somewhere between the first word and the last word.

Making sentences, phrases, and paragraphs concise takes practice and a slightly masochistic tendency to deflate one's own ego. The author can use a nasty red pen (or the equally nasty delete key on the word processor keyboard) to eliminate extra words and phrases but still retain the basic information. The goal is to make the writing simple, a concept that actually frustrates some MIS professionals. But words are only tools with which to communicate, and there is nothing intrinsically mystical about them. If a thought can be expressed in ten words, why use twenty? From a purely businesslike standpoint, it is more efficient to write and then have someone read ten words than twenty. Cutting unnecessary words is an easy way to improve writing that is wordy or overly confusing.

Clarity involves the choice of words. An otherwise routine piece of writing can suddenly become a dynamic communication device when the author examines the vocabulary and replaces dull words with more exciting ones. No, an MIS document is not designed to elicit passion or incite people to revolution, but it should never be boring.

In some respects, words are like people—some are positive, definite, and exciting, whereas others are negative, unclear, or boring. Consider this summary of a new online order entry system that cost a company $500,000 and a massive overtime effort by programmers, analysts, and users:

The new online system should reduce the processing time from customer to shipping, decrease the number of errors, and lower our inventory.

The information may be accurate, but the board of directors may wonder silently at the results of its $500,000 investment. The programmers, analysts, and users, who have given up many nights and weekends, may share that feeling of concern. Just a few additional words (and specific rather than general facts) will make the system seem worth the time, money, and extra effort:

The new online order entry system will slash the total processing time, from the initial phone call to shipping, by 500 percent, virtually eliminate out-of-stock situations in the warehouse, and reduce our inventory investment by at least 3 percent.

The difference between the two examples is striking because the second illustration uses both *positive adjectives* and *measurable facts*. These two simple techniques in combination can increase the clarity of any piece of writing.

Clarity suffers when the author uses too many buzzwords that are never defined. Any long document that contains many technical or business terms should have a glossary or adequate definitions spread throughout the document itself. Assuming that the reader will know the current buzzwords, abbreviations, or complex business terms is often dangerous. Even communicating within the MIS organization is difficult, as system software professionals seem to use an entirely different language than business systems analysts, and it may be that neither group understands the terminology of microcomputers. And MIS employees may not understand the data collection terminology of the manufacturing plant, or the sophisticated budgeting manipulations necessary during the year-end closing. If a memo or proposal is to be clear, the terminology must be explained.

Abbreviations are also confusing, since the information systems community has gone wild over the benefits of abbreviating words and phrases. When there is any doubt about the meaning of a buzzword or abbreviation, the author should always define the term. If a reader does not understand one or two key words, the author has failed in the attempt to communicate. One word can indeed make the difference!

2.4 SUMMARY OF KEY POINTS

☐ Effective writing is simply another skill that can be learned.

☐ The most important requirement is the ability to constructively criticize your own work.

☐ Before you start to write, you must plan ahead:
Make your ideas logical.
Analyze the needs and characteristics of your audience.
Define all terms clearly.

☐ Style is important in technical writing. One relatively easy way to achieve a positive style is to make your writing seem natural.

☐ Five rules for natural writing are:
Use formal conversations as a model.
Be honest with yourself and your readers.
Anticipate questions and provide answers in the text.
Use examples that your audience will understand.
Vary the sentence structure to avoid boring the reader (and yourself).

☐ The first draft is only a start. Review your work carefully and pretend you are the audience. Examine each sentence and paragraph for clarity. Look for ways to express the same thought in fewer words. Try for tight, concise writing. Use positive, active words, and include measurable facts as often as possible.

☐ Two good references are:
Skees, William D.: *Writing Handbook for Computer Professionals,* Lifetime Learning Publications, Belmont, Calif., 1982, pp. 11–59.
Van Duyn, J.: *The DP Professional's Guide to Writing Effective Technical Communication,* John Wiley & Sons, New York, 1982, pp. 13–33.

chapter **3**

Project Development Documents

INTRODUCTION

Developing a new system or modifying an existing one is an exciting and challenging opportunity, but many such projects are not successful. They may be late, over budget, or incomplete or may ultimately cause more problems than they solve. One solution is to improve the quality of every document produced during the development cycle. Without good, carefully designed documents, management can expect errors, mistakes, and misunderstandings. This chapter presents eight important documents that can be used in virtually any development methodology. Systems analysts, technical writers, and users will find this chapter a one-source guide for high-quality, efficient, and accurate documents. Managers responsible for development projects should also review this chapter—they will find a wealth of answers to their project management problems!

A standard joke in data-processing circles is that professionals who have the least to do with a large, important project get promotions, whereas the rest find new jobs! Is project management always that complicated? Is MIS management doomed to suffer with late projects, angry users, and frustrated professionals? The answer is a definite no. The ultimate solution may involve more user participation, online prototyping, and faster development techniques, but one basic prerequisite is *high-quality project development documentation that follows a logical, management-oriented policy*. The best methodology in the world will not succeed with poor written documentation.

3.1 THE PROJECT LIFE CYCLE

Volumes have been written, consultants have gotten rich, and wars have been fought over which is the "best" project-development methodology. In the late 1970s and early 1980s such arguments peaked, and many experienced project managers now follow one of two paths. Either they routinely select the one they are most familiar with or they develop their own variation based on the current situation. Perhaps all methodologies are correct; the difference lies not so much in *which* one is used as in *how* it is implemented.

They have one factor in common: most of them are implemented via the written word. If it is implemented well, the project has a chance for success. If it is not implemented well, the project and its staff are on the road to disaster.

This chapter describes eight documents for use with several popular approaches to project development:

1. Proposal or concept document
2. Feasibility statement
3. Business plan
4. Functional specifications
5. System design

6. Cost-benefits analysis
7. Programming specifications
8. Project history or "chrono" file

Large or complex projects may need all eight documents, but other projects may skip one or more steps in the development cycle. These documents are *recommendations* rather than absolute necessities. Project managers must decide on a case-by-case basis which steps (and corresponding documents) are justified on the basis of their knowledge, experience, understanding, and perception of the project complexity. Another key factor is often "degree of risk." The more steps a manager skips in the formal development cycle, the greater the risk of failure.

For example, a written cost-benefits analysis might show that computerizing shipping manager Terry Transit's daily schedule will cost $20,000. But if department clerk Alan Axle does the same job with his cardex file in seven minutes every day, one must immediately question the value of the project. A cost of $20,000 in analyst and programmer time will pay for many seven-minute efforts by Alan. Unless there are other benefits—such as greater accuracy or future integration into other systems—the project may not be justified. Without a formal cost-benefits document, management could easily make the wrong decision. *Good documentation practices lead directly to good management decisions.*

One can always go to extremes by insisting that every request follow the complete series of steps. If accounting manager Lana Ledger wanted three more lines printed on each page of the trial balance report, the MIS director could require a concept document, feasibility statement, business plan, functional specifications, cost-benefits analysis, system design, programming specifications, and project history file. Or the director could simply call Charley Cobol and ask him to increase the line count by three. An MIS director with any sense would choose the second approach. *Too much documentation is just as bad as not enough.*

3.2 THE PROPOSAL OR CONCEPT DOCUMENT

The *proposal* is the official document that triggers the project development cycle. Most MIS professionals never realize that a simple user request—even if scribbled on a napkin from the company cafeteria—is simply a preliminary version of the formal proposal. Both documents are methods of asking for assistance from MIS, although the proposal is a more defined document that requires a formal response. The purpose of a proposal is to explain the need, estimated scope, and possible design for a new project or a major enhancement to the current application systems.

Who should write the proposal? Should it be the user or an MIS professional? The best results are obtained when users and MIS staff members jointly create the document. It is irrelevant which department claims official ownership. In the 1980s, as user participation becomes an absolute necessity rather than simply a "nice-to-have" idea, joint user-MIS cooperation at the start of a project is vital. Even the most sophisticated users typically have only one-fourth the information necessary for a good proposal, and MIS employees have another fourth. The interaction between the two groups can help discover the missing 50 percent.

Proposals should include any damaging information as well as the more obvious goods news. If shipping manager Terry Transit wants his freight payments procedure computerized but knows that in two years the company will be considering an accounting package that may include freight control, he should mention that possibility. Any fact or future event that makes the concept less justified or more complicated should be mentioned, since bad news will eventually surface.

3.2.1 Open Access to MIS during the Proposal-Writing Stage

Successful proposals require that users have access to an MIS manager, programmer, or analyst during the blue-sky stage of the project life cycle. Senior MIS management should understand that allowing such access for dreaming is actually more cost-effective than keeping users away from the MIS staff, because it helps reduce the wasted effort when users propose unjustified or even impossible ideas. It is easier to catch the errors before they go into the MIS pipeline and demand precious management attention and resources. Users working in a vacuum may create empty ideas in the same way that the MIS staff working in a vacuum may create equally empty ideas. Conversely, either group can miss simple alternatives that will solve their immediate needs. When Mary Markdown in Merchandising has a brilliant idea but cannot share her thoughts with a technical analyst, she may come up with the following proposal:

> Buyers and their assistants spend a lot of time looking for negative stock balances and negative costs. We spend most of Monday morning just scanning each report to catch minus numbers, to which we give priority. I suggest that inventory reports be changed so that any negative number prints in red rather than in black ink. This will save the merchandise staff many hours of tedious work. When can you have it ready?

Since most high-speed line printers today use only black ink, the concept is not feasible. Had Mary worked with systems analyst Frank Flowchart, the two would have proposed a more reasonable solution of a separate report for negative numbers. Mary did not use her time efficiently because she did not have access to an MIS professional for blue-sky thinking.

Even when users have good ideas, without MIS counsel they may fail to communicate essential facts. Consider this proposal for a purchases reconciliation system written by a very frustrated accounts payable supervisor:

> When invoices come into the accounts payable system, I have a hard time deciding whether to pay them immediately or verify them first. How do I know whether Interna-

tional Screws really sent forty cases of number 6 steel screws? If I call Fran Fastner in Purchasing, she will say, "That was two months ago. I can't remember. I can't recall every shipment. Do I look like an elephant?" If I call Peter Pallet in the warehouse he will say, "We marked the receipt two months ago. I don't remember whether there were really forty cases. I can't remember those details. Do I look like an elephant?"

It's true I get copies of most receipts, but they come in randomly, some are illegible, and I miss almost one-fourth of them. I would need four more clerks just to manually match receipts against invoices.

The problem is real, but the proposal does not communicate factually. The reader thinks, "But tell me more!" This paper should be interpreted as a call for help rather than a formal proposal! With a little help from an MIS analyst, the request could be rewritten as follows.

When many invoices come into Accounts Payable, we have no way of verifying that the warehouse actually received all the merchandise being billed. For example, if we get a bill for forty cases, we don't know whether the warehouse actually received forty cases. We manually match only those invoices and receipts over $7,000, so the majority never get checked.

Since the computer has captured receipts in the inventory system, can you enter invoices and match them against receipts? We would then pay every matching invoice and investigate any discrepancy beyond a variable dollar amount. We need that amount variable by vendor because we suspect that some manufacturers routinely overbill us.

3.2.2 Adding Justification to a Proposal

The preceding document touches both sides of an idea, but one vital ingredient is missing: Why *do* the project? Where is the justification? A more experienced systems analyst could rewrite the document in such a way as to force any cost-conscious reader to stand up and cheer:

> The majority of invoices that come to Accounts Payable are paid without question—only invoices with a total dollar value over $7,000 are routinely matched with warehouse receipts. Last year Wonderful Widgets paid over $3.2 million on invoices that were never verified. Since most vendors know our lack of payment control, we are open for widespread cheating. Assuming an overcharge rate of only 1 percent, we overpaid $32,000 last year.
>
> The inventory control system already captures receipts and adjustments. If we created a perpetual file of invoices sorted by invoice number and date, we could match all receipts against invoices on a weekly basis. This new system should catch all deliberate overcharges and errors.

This last version has the spark of *justification,* which will even excite the company president! A proposal should tell the reader *why* the idea is important. In fact, the author has deliberately understated the case: a 1 percent overcharge rate assumes that 99 percent of the vendors are honest. What if the rate is really 3 percent? Then Wonderful Widgets lost $96,000 instead of $32,000! And the problem continues every year. Think about the impact on the bottom line! A good proposal requires some degree of sales savvy, but authors should stay on the side of conservatism.

3.2.3   The Complete Proposal Package

Along with the proposal itself, the complete package should contain a cover memo and an appendix, and together they should answer the following questions:

1. What is the business or scientific problem?
2. Is the problem important enough to be solved by computer?

3. Why can't it be handled by the current procedures or systems?
4. What should the computer solution include?
5. Who has been involved in the proposal preparation?
6. When does the solution have to be implemented?

The following cover memo helps answer these questions:

FROM: Joyce Journal, AP Supervisor
TO: Mark Muscle, Vice President
SUBJECT: Accounts Reconciliation Problem

Attached is the proposal for computerizing the matching of our invoices and receipts. As you know, Wonderful Widgets may be overpaying a tremendous amount on invoices less than $7,000, but we have absolutely no way of knowing for sure. The proposal is a product of the combined effort of Lana Ledger, myself, and Frank Flowchart from MIS.

Our heavy purchasing period comes in May. If we have the computerized matching in place by April, it could have a large effect on next year's bottom line.

I will set up a meeting later this month to discuss the proposal and any questions you may have.

Thank you.

The appendix attached to a proposal may seem out of place, especially when it includes technical notes in mysterious data-processing jargon. But the very act of contemplating an idea or suggestion with a user often generates details about justification, cost, design problems, advantages, and disadvantages that will be useful in the future. Unless such potentially valuable tidbits are preserved on paper, they may be forgotten, and the company will lose its investment in employee time. Raw, hastily edited notes are not impressive, but adding them to the proposal keeps them alive for the next set of players. *One of the basic purposes of technical writing is to preserve knowledge gained on company time.*

3.3 THE FEASIBILITY STATEMENT

After the proposal is made, the first task faced by MIS management is to evaluate the feasiblity of the proposal as it relates to the organization as a whole. The outcome of this analysis is expressed in a short but vital document called the *feasibility statement.* The purpose of this paper is to either recommend some form of continued action or suggest stopping the project. Good project management requires that MIS take a stand early! *Creating the feasibility statement may be the most ignored step in the entire system development life cycle.*

A common complaint from senior managers is that MIS spends considerable time on ideas or proposals that eventually prove too costly, too undefined, or simply not practical. Even worse is the classic explanation given by the frustrated MIS professional who casually admits, "Well, we knew it wasn't feasible three months ago when we first talked about it." Then why did the company spend three months investigating that idea? Perhaps because MIS management does not routinely insist on a feasibility statement for every proposal!

Human resources today are simply too valuable to waste on ideas or concepts that will obviously never see the light of day. Even internal corporate political considerations no longer justify working on ideas that are not valid.

3.3.1 Writing Simple and Complex Feasibility Statements

The characteristics of the feasibility statement depend on the complexity of the concept and the outcome of the analysis. If no research is needed or the concept is obviously both practical and worthwhile, the statement will be short and simple. But to examine the feasibility of a purchases reconciliation system, one may study the current inventory system (receipt information), discuss the possibility of a new master file (to capture invoices), and work with the probable users (to determine the reporting requirements). The final answer may be: Yes, it seems feasible in our environment with current hardware. If, however, the idea is good but hardware resource limitations make it impractical without a major hardware investment, the recommendation may be negative. The feasibility statement needs enough supporting evidence to convince an objective third party that the recommendation is fair.

An effective feasibility statement for the purchases reconciliation system might be:

The proposal for an automated purchases reconciliation system appears reasonable. Since the inventory control system captures all receipts, we now have exactly half the required data. According to a rough estimate (based on last year's invoices), the current data entry staff could absorb the load of entering all AP invoices if this were done on a daily, noncritical basis. However, we should be prepared to add at least one full-time operator to handle priority AP batches. Alternatively, the new online general ledger package could be used to capture invoices with slight modifications. Since we have never worked with purchases reconciliation reports, we must spend large amounts of time designing the reports and be prepared for major changes once the system is in production. With the new system in operation, we should have no trouble running several new weekend jobs after the final inventory control update and reporting job streams.

We considered buying the module available from the general ledger vendor, but our specialized receiving procedures would require costly modifications of any purchased package. Therefore, we should write the system in-house.

In our opinion, the proposed purchases reconciliation system is both useful and feasible from a business standpoint. Although it is impossible to estimate the cost, I predict on the basis of previous experience that the cost of developing a reconciliation system will be roughly comparable to the cost of developing the expense-tracking system created in 1984.

Most readers would generally agree with the conclusions and suggest continuing the project (which actually means adding it to the MIS priority list). Yet the feasibility statement does not paint a completely happy picture. It mentions the need to add additional data entry staff members to handle other critical work that will be displaced. It warns about major changes in the reporting structure once the system is complete. A good feasibility statement must cover both sides of the question.

Systems analysts dislike the fact that managers often demand project development estimates before the team has even started the design phase! In the preceding example, the author has cleverly avoided giving a number but has given management a reference point that is almost as good by comparing the new proposal to a completed project. *The feasibility statement should not include cost estimates, but the author should provide some indication of the cost for management.* Such comparisons are often the best way to communicate scope, effort, and probable cost.

3.3.2 Writing a Feasibility Statement with No Immediate Recommendation

What happens when the systems analyst develops more questions than answers? The purpose of the feasibility statement then changes. Rather than serving as a definite recommendation, the feasibility statement should become a "road map" to the next decision point. The purpose is not to avoid an immediate decision; rather it is to provide management with a plan for making the best possible choice. *As technology increases in complexity, feasibility statements themselves will become more difficult.* If the analyst team cannot make a recommendation, it can at least suggest ways to eventually make a recommendation.

A common situation in today's complex technical environment is one in which the evaluating team members need more research before they can provide any recommendation. In effect, they are confident they can suggest the best alternative, but they need additional resources or analysis time. Companies that are considering a decision-support system (DSS), for example, may find it difficult to judge its true feasibility unless they have in-house expertise with DSS packages and their use. The initial feasibility statement should honestly admit this lack of knowledge, but not quite in the blunt manner chosen by the new systems analyst Tina Template:

> After examining the proposal for a decision-support system submitted by Vice President of Sales "Honest John" Jones, I am stumped! I've never worked with a decision support system. After reading the brochures I am even more confused about their value. The cost is astronomical! We could hire three more full-time programmers for what the package costs. Is it feasible? I wish I knew!

After an unpleasant talk with her boss, the statement could be rewritten in a more professional manner:

> After studying the proposal for a decision-support system (DSS) submitted by Vice President of Sales "Honest John" Jones, I recommend that a team of MIS and sales department staff members examine the brochures and some additional material I will provide. A good DSS package is very expensive, and many complex factors help decide whether the purchase is feasible. Since no one in the company has worked with a true DSS, we are all in a new area.
>
> I suggest the MIS managers select a financial systems analyst and a programming supervisor to meet with Honest John or his designates. After an estimated six one-hour sessions, the team should give one of three recommendations:
>
> 1. The probable benefits are not worth the cost, at least at this time.
> 2. The idea is interesting, but a long-range research plan is needed.

3. The benefits appear justified, and we need an action plan to select the best package.

Tina's second version implies exactly what her first document stated—she is baffled! But it now provides a logical plan or road map to reach the next logical milestone. It is perfectly acceptable for the feasibility statement to say, "I don't know." It is not acceptable for the feasibility statement to stop at that point. The author must suggest the next move.

3.3.3   Business Factors in Feasibility Statements

Deciding whether a plan is feasible or infeasible involves many variables. For example, consider a retail buyer who is thoroughly pleased with her "interactive file maintenance system" and now wants an "interactive purchase order system." The MIS feasibility statement is:

> Freda Fashion's proposed interactive purchase order system would be a great help to the entire buying staff. There is no doubt about the technical feasibility. Yet before we commit additional resources to a design effort, we need to understand the implications of this proposal.
>
> Systems Software is already investigating a data-base package to integrate all merchandising applications. The interactive file maintenance system was our first attempt at a CICS system, and it uses a special minifile that actually passes transactions to the nightly batch update. To generate online purchase orders, we must create three additional minifiles and then duplicate the processing during the overnight runs. We are already having serious control problems with the first minifile, and several more could cause additional production errors.
>
> Technically, we can bring up a CICS minipurchase order system within a few months, but this means allocating our limited CICS expertise to specific applications rather than to the already proposed and approved unified merchandise control system.

Although the statement is clearly slanted toward a rejection, the writer has not formally expressed an opinion. The MIS director is free to consider the economic and political benefits without worrying about the technical issues. The author has stressed business concerns that may make the project unjustifiable. The feasibility statement can include virtually anything that has a significant bearing on the practicality and value of the proposal. Analysts should open their minds to the business and political worlds around them as well as the more familiar technical arena. Even the factor of "lost opportunities" is valid for consideration if the author remembers that the primary assignment is to concentrate on evaluating one specific idea at a time.

3.3.4 Guidelines for Saying No

Writing style and content are critical when delivering negative recommendations. Consider a feasibility statement written by the new systems analyst Tina Template:

> The proposed automatic freight payment system does sound promising, but other factors make the idea infeasible. First, the freight clerk, Willy Wheel, cannot even turn on his typewriter without help, let alone operate a microcomputer. Terry Transit smokes those big, smelly cigars that will foul up any electronic device. Also, he has a nasty habit of kicking both people and equipment when they do not function according to his standards. Finally, those truck drivers I met could never stop long enough during the day to enter their own rate codes. Unless the people in the shipping department are fired, I do not feel that a computerized freight payment system is practical at Wonderful Widgets.

Tina will never win friends and influence people with her statement. Yet she may have discovered serious considerations that make the proposal impractical. The staff may not be able to handle a microcomputer, and the truck drivers may find it troublesome or too time-consuming to enter their own rate codes when they are rushing to meet tight schedules. But this same information can be communicated in a less insulting manner:

> The proposed automatic freight payment system on a microcomputer does sound useful, but we have uncovered certain problems. The office staff has never worked with CRTs. The office itself is not air-conditioned or humidity-controlled, and smoke from cigarettes and pipes can damage sensitive electronic equipment. The truck drivers may find it difficult to enter codes, since they are typically on very tight schedules with less than ten minutes per changeover. If we are willing to address these problems in detail, we should consider the project at some later date.

Although the first version is more colorful and does accurately describe the shipping department environment, the second effort conveys the same information in a more professional manner. If the MIS director wishes to visit the shipping office, he can personally observe Terry Transit smoking a big, smelly cigar and kicking the file cabinet when a drawer sticks. He can casually notice Willy Wheel spending five minutes looking for the "power" switch on his electric typewriter. He can be pushed out of the way by burly truck drivers rushing madly to their new assignments. But this tactful feasibility statement lets all parties blame the rejection on the cost of air conditioning and lack of CRT experience. No one is insulted, and Tina Template does not have to face a large, angry shipping manager smoking a big, smelly cigar. If an idea must be rejected for personnel reasons, the author should provide a reasonable excuse in the public document that will satisfy the human ego. Truth in technical writing is important, but not at the cost of bruised egos and damaged relationships. Even large, angry shipping managers have feelings.

3.4 THE BUSINESS PLAN

Business plans are not only for multimillion-dollar projects. Even relatively small projects that are complex, that require capital expenditures above a certain amount, or that appear to be high-risk deserve a separate document *that analyzes both the development effort and the project itself from a business standpoint.* So-called business plans that describe only the project or only the development effort will leave many questions unaddressed. Good business plans are difficult to write, but they are key documents that often separate the failures from the successes. The business plan—sometimes known as a "sanity check"—is management's "control knob" on MIS activities.

A complete business plan has seven sections:

1. Executive summary
2. Scope
3. Assumptions and open issues
4. Objectives
5. Interfaces
6. Resources and plan for next stage
7. Estimated timetable

Even the most comprehensive business plan is usually less than fifteen or twenty pages in length. Considering human nature, documents over that length tend to be ignored, returned to the "in" basket, or simply put aside. By keeping the paper relatively short and adopting a businesslike approach to the material, the author will communicate successfully to a greater number of readers. Except in the assumptions and open issues section, the document should stay with generalities rather than specifics. *A business plan is the road map that tells MIS where to go and how to get there.* It is more of a procedural document than an informational one.

Mechanical preparation is also important. Since senior-level managers are accustomed to professionally prepared documents, such as sales brochures, the author should use the best printing, cover, and folder available. Even the title page should be impressive. Selling ability is an important factor in most technical writing assignments, but the business plan requires extra effort.

3.4.1 Sections of the Business Plan

The *executive summary* describes the project, estimated resources, development approach, and both potential benefits and problems. It is two pages or less in length and is written as a stand-alone document. The summary should be the most polished section in the business plan.

The *scope* sets the official boundaries and limitations for the project team. It answers the twin questions: How far will the project go, and what will the project encompass? This section also defines the responsibilities of the project team as perceived by the author. Merely stating these perceptions will often generate fascinating discussions and should help prevent future misunderstandings.

The *assumptions and open issues* section lists the major assumptions that have been identified in previous discussions and significant open issues that must be resolved. Critical open questions may later affect the scope, cost, and benefits of the entire project. The business plan does not settle those issues, but simply identifies them for management attention. The business plan for a development project offers a perfect opportunity to place important matters before senior management in a nonthreatening manner.

The *objectives* section describes the purpose and goals of the project. Like the assumptions and open issues portion, this section will help all parties understand the perceived purpose of the project. As organizations become more complex, the search for a common set of goals, even in seemingly obvious projects, becomes equally complex.

The *interfaces* section lists the application systems, departments, and operating units that will directly or indirectly interface with the project. The purpose of this information is to alert other personnel that their assistance may be required in the future. As many MIS managers have discovered, one of the most embarrassing mistakes of the systems development cycle is the interface that was forgotten!

The *resources and plan for next stage* section lists the people and computer resources needed for subsequent phases of the project. Although the business plan occurs too early in the development cycle for definite resource commitments, the author should attempt to quantify the needed support. Management wants some indication of required analyst, programmer, and user effort as well as some opinion concerning machine utilization.

The *estimated timetable or calendar* identifies all the major developmental milestones of the development and installation program.

3.4.2 Managing the Business Plan

A business plan should never be submitted as a "surprise" to MIS or company management! At least one draft must be circulated to selected individuals before the first official version is published, and their comments or suggestions should be carefully considered. Not only will those changes help clarify the document, but incorporating even minor suggestions is an excellent way to make those readers feel a sense of ownership toward the business plan. People will instinctively search for "their" comments or ideas. Human nature is complicated, but it can be used to the author's advantage. The writer is not being dishonest or sneaky—it is good sense to incorporate reasonable suggestions from people who must approve the document anyway. It is equally good sense to understand how this process affects many readers.

The information in the business plan will seldom remain untouched, as if etched in stone. Rather, as new facts or possibilities are discovered in the requirements and system design phases, the author will revise the business plan. *An out-of-date business plan is worse than no business plan at all.* Even organizations change, and the longer the term of the project, the more opportunity for changes that affect every on-going development project. Those new directions and policies cannot be ignored, because the business plan is probably the most publicized document outside MIS. The business plan must be updated as the situation changes.

Updating the business plan on a word processor is relatively simple, but each change should be marked by either an indicator in the margin, a change page that tells the reader which sections and paragraphs have been modified, or both. Section 3.6 describes these techniques in detail.

The decision to include costs in a business plan depends on the organization's philosophy. Many senior managers insist that any paper with the title "business plan" address the cost issue, at least for budgeting purposes. Although the business plan is formulated early in the development cycle, the author can estimate both development and ongoing costs. Of course, when the project changes or as more details are filled in, the cost data must be revised.

3.5 THE REQUIREMENTS DOCUMENT

A requirements document may be called *functional specifications, user requirements,* or *user definition.* Whatever the name, the purpose of the requirements document is to define the project's needs from the viewpoint of both the user and MIS. Requirements documents that consider only user needs and ignore technical considerations are often confusing and incomplete, and requirements documents that concentrate only on the MIS aspects are even worse.

The format and length of the document varies according to the complexity and scope of the project, but most requirements documents include the following topics:

1. Overview and purpose
2. Input
3. Processing
4. Output
5. Integration considerations (including data-base relationships)
6. Timing and operational factors
7. Hardware requirements
8. Appendix

3.5.1 Sections of the Requirements Document

The *overview* states the purpose of the proposed application or system and the scope of the project (taken from the business plan) and briefly describes the major functions.

Acceptable requirements documents can vary from 5-page summaries to several 500-page volumes. Therefore the overview should contain a statement that explains the level of detail and how the team came to choose that level. If there is no explicit statement, the reader will naturally assume that the requirements are complete. This may be incorrect and lead to a serious misunderstanding! Yet specifying the level of detail is simple. The overview may state: The user requirements in this document are complete as we currently see them. Another version could be: The information in this paper presents only general user requirements, and the design phase will further define additional requirements. Both sentences let the reader know exactly what to expect.

If the project deals with a typical business application, the *input* section describes the batch, online, or machine-collected transactions. If the proposal concerns a new computer, the input section would discuss such factors as operating control parameters or electronic components that regulate the system. Even many "exotic" MIS projects have input requirements, even if they are not immediately apparent. For most business-type applications, this section answers the question: What will the user give the system?

Processing summarizes the computer manipulations of data and the relationships among data elements. In an inventory control system, for example, the processing section would contain formulas in user-understandable terms to calculate the final cost of items received at the warehouse.

The *output* section describes reports or cathode-ray tube (CRT) screen formats that reflect the combination of input data and processing. A summary of hard-copy reports should include such aspects as availability (daily, weekly, monthly, yearly, or on request), headings, columns, and important data fields. If the system includes a user-oriented report writer, the analyst should help create sample report formats. Even the ad hoc inquiry feature needs at least one or two examples. CRT screens should be described so that the users can appreciate the very critical "human engineering" aspects of an online system.

Missing from many requirements documents is the purpose behind output reports or screens. Simply asking a user to define each purpose often initiates a dialog that helps both the user and the MIS analyst. For example, after MIS has spent ten weeks creating the new "overstock report," exactly how will it be used by the buyers and warehouse staff? Has the user defined the procedures necessary to derive maximum benefit from this new report? Is it usable? If not, what other information is needed? *The output section of the requirements document will be the starting point for the user manual!*

When considering changes to an existing system, the *integration* section is often the most important. Many errors in development projects are caused by a failure to define interface points and the snowball effect resulting from last-minute changes. Even data-base–oriented shops may still have integration problems. The author must not rely only on the MIS technical wizards—sophisticated users often have special insight that will help the analyst team define those integration points.

Timing and operational factors are important if they are not specifically described in the input or processing sections. Some user requirements lose their value as the time between the input and output increases. In other situations, the timing is dictated by external demands, such as accounting calendars or machine availability. Some analysts label this section "project limitations."

The document needs a section on *hardware requirements* if the proposed idea demands specialized hardware or software. Today most business-application systems generally develop their hardware requirements as part of the system design phase.

The *appendix* is a vital section that includes supporting material of every kind. Random notes concerning user needs, design requirements, or potential implementation problems are perfect candidates for the appendix. Sometimes an author discovers other papers or detailed explanations that are inappropriate in the body of the document but will be needed in subsequent development stages. The appendix is simply a mechanism for storing valuable knowledge gained during the requirements phase and passing that information to other workers.

3.5.2 The Three-Layer Approach to Requirements

In each section, the requirements should be categorized into three relative levels: absolute, recommended, and optional. A requirements document that simply lists requirements and does not differentiate among them fails in its mission. *Not all requirements are alike—some are vital, some are important, and others are merely wishful dreams.* The author can separate the important from the less important by classifying every requirement according to the following definitions:

> *Absolute:* Requirements without which the project is virtually useless
>
> *Recommended:* Requirements that are wanted by the user (or MIS), but without which the project is still useful
>
> *Optional:* Requirements that are nice to have, but are not critical to the project design

Both recommended and optional requirements are subject to later negotiation. If, for example, an optional requirement is later found to cost half as much as the rest of the design, the project team can legitimately suggest dropping that requirement. However, experienced systems analysts seldom use the word "negotiable" when explaining the three-layered approach to requirements definition.

Users who have never seen this format may stubbornly insist that everything they ask for is absolutely essential to the project, the corporation, and the entire planet Earth. Their attitude is exaggerated but understandable if they have previously suffered through incomplete or late projects. Users may worry that MIS will immediately forget every requirement not classified as absolute. The MIS management team should carefully point out that by defining the degree of need in the requirements document, MIS hopes to avoid such battles. Furthermore, asking a user to make those judgments on a case-by-case basis during the more time-critical programming process is both unfair and inaccurate. The best time for making difficult value judgments is during the requirements phase, when the user is conceptualizing the entire system at one time.

3.6   SYSTEM DESIGN DOCUMENTATION

If the functional specifications tell the reader *what* and the business plan tells the reader *why*, the system design answers the final question, *how*.

The purpose of a system design is to combine information from the requirements document, feasibility statement, and business plan to create the best solution for the organization. In some situations, if the needs of the organization will override the needs of specific users, the design document should be honest enough to reflect that consideration. A good design team will consider at least thirteen important factors:

1. User needs
2. MIS environment
3. Cost considerations
4. Technical requirements
5. Company policies
6. Other projects planned or in progress
7. Customs
7. Estimated life cycle of the system
9. Risk value
10. Availability of resources
11. Degree of user participation
12. Political importance in the organization
13. Implementation schedule or timing requirements

3.6.1 Unique Characteristics of Design Documents

The technical writer must understand three important differences between other MIS documents and a true system design. First, the system design must be *easy to change.* Second, the design should be written with almost *standalone sections.* Third, the text must contain numerous *references to other sections* to help the reader locate additional information.

The business plan and requirements document are relatively stable. They may be issued several times as major changes are made to the scope or purpose of the project, but those documents are generally fixed. The systems design, however, is a *working document* that is meant to change. The first version may be literally torn apart by users, MIS technicians, and managers. The second version may suffer even worse treatment. There is nothing wrong with critical comments—in fact, they prove that readers are taking the design seriously!

The second difference is that other project documents are written as an integrated whole, but a systems design must serve as a reference document and therefore should contain virtually stand-alone sections. For example, the programmer needs only one place in which to search for detailed facts and will dislike spending hours searching through a 100-page document looking for needed information about a specific topic. Whereas the business plan or requirements document may be studied once or twice, the systems design will be used continually during the project by a wide variety of readers. It never goes away. It may ultimately be cursed or praised, but it lives forever.

Creating sections or chapters that are almost standalone is a new and frustrating challenge for many authors. Writers normally create papers that do not repeat information or facts. They want their document to become a cohesive whole. But a system design document is never a candidate for a creative writing award. A business plan should be compared to a beautiful work of art that communicates in smooth, flowing language, whereas the systems design document is a very dull, but necessary, set of blueprints. There are techniques to liven up a design document, but material as dull as blueprints will never make good bedtime reading. To create stand-alone sections, the author must include enough material in each logical unit for the reader to have all the necessary information in that section. The writer must occasionally repeat detail already found in other units and must provide complete explanations throughout the text. Lana Ledger may not enjoy reading about the LIFO inventory posting process that she designed three years ago, but a programmer/analyst reading a design for inventory valuation needs complete information. *A systems design with stand-alone sections will dramatically help the programming, systems, and user staff members who must work with the design document.*

Even when the author has done a truly outstanding job of creating stand-alone sections, some readers will invariably need more information. It is impossible to repeat everything every reader may eventually need. Therefore, the system design document should contain in the text specific references to other chapters or units. For example, if the design for an integrated manufacturing system mentions the effects of government regulations in several places, each instance should point directly (by title and section number) to the chapter on government regulation. It is more efficient for the knowledgeable author to provide the pointers to related material than to have the readers search the document themselves. The goal of an effective system design document is to communicate *easily* by saving the reader time and effort.

3.6.2 The Level of Detail

Two very good design documents may have different levels of detail. One may be a massive volume that contains every known fact about the project, whereas the other equally successful document may present only enough information for the next stage of the project. The latter approach assumes that some of the design effort can be left to the programmers or programmer/analysts. There is no absolute guideline, but the level of detail must be determined on a logical basis for that particular project. That is, the authors or department managers cannot simply ignore the question and hope for the best. The analyst team should never choose the level of detail on the basis of the toss of a coin, the degree of management pressure, or the next impending deadline. Rather, the decision can be made by answering several important questions:

1. Will the project team use traditional programming techniques or will they implement fourth-generation development tools?
2. Will the project be developed in-house or by an outside group?
3. Are the developers familiar with the application or business concepts? Are they senior- or junior-level people?
4. How much effort can the users realistically donate to the programming phase?
5. Will the original systems analyst be heavily involved in the programming?
6. Does the design contain any new technical concepts?
7. What degree of risk does the project have?
8. Are the users cooperative?
9. Is management flexible enough to leave some unanswered issues for the detailed programming stages?

When the analyst team members have answered these questions, they can intelligently plan the level of detail required in their specific project.

3.6.3 Graphics and Text

The best design documents use both graphics and text, because each appeals to a different type of readers. Flow charts, diagrams, and graphic symbols are excellent methods for portraying relationships, whereas text seems to better communicate specific information. Human nature also plays a part. Some people simply prefer graphics, whereas others ignore pictures and go straight to the written word. A document that uses both techniques has a better chance of communicating effectively to more readers. Although graphics are becoming more popular (because of the microcomputer explosion and the excellent graphics capability of some word-processing systems), text will always be important. A document that relies only on symbols will lose many readers. Likewise, another document that ignores the value of graphics will lose an opportunity to communicate, because text alone may not always do the job.

One common graphic tool is the classic *hierarchical-input-process-output* (HIPO) method developed by IBM. Some authors have developed variations such as the *input-process-output* (IPO) method. HIPO analyzes a system in terms of specific user input, computer processing, and resultant output. Although MIS departments differ in their implementation of HIPO charts, most MIS professionals use a format with three horizontal or vertical areas labeled "Input," "Process," and "Output." HIPO charts work well when the author can portray the system logic in hierarchical terms, since the initial (or level-1) HIPO chart can summarize each function as it relates to the general system flow. Each succeeding HIPO diagram then analyzes a function or process in more detail.

Standard flowchart symbols will also work if the audience is familiar with their purpose. In practice, systems analysts typically choose either the graphics tool they have personally worked with or the method designated the MIS standard.

If the decision is made to use any form of graphics, the author should be consistent. That is, if the first of five major logical topics has data-flow diagrams, the other four topics should have similar charts. Any inconsistency will leave the reader puzzled and will ultimately hurt the communication process.

3.6.4 Sections of a Design Document

Contrary to the dreams of some managers, there is no perfect format or organization for every system design document. Rather, the analyst team must start with a complete list of topics or sections and create an individualized structure for each document. The differing needs of each project invariably require a slightly unique organization. Complex system designs may use all the recommended sections (and perhaps additional topics), whereas another project may need only a few items. *It is unrealistic to force all design documents to follow a rigid, unchangeable standard format.* They should follow similar guidelines, but the author needs some degree of freedom. The following list is only a guide to help analysts quickly determine *what* topics should be covered and in what sequence.

A complete design document for a complex MIS business application may contain the following sections:

1. Informational pages
2. Summary
3. Assumptions and guidelines
4. Overall system flow
5. Inputs
6. Processing logic
7. Outputs
8. Error conditions
9. Hardware, software, and personnel requirements
10. Interfaces with existing systems
11. Appendix
    a. User responsibilities
    b. Timing considerations
    c. Technical notes
    d. Potential problems and drawbacks
    e. Summary of rejected alternatives
    f. Cost estimates
    g. Development timetable
    h. Definitions
    i. Miscellaneous

Design documents that propose a new product use a different format:

1. Product summary and features
2. Market survey and current competition
3. Sales and marketing strategy
4. Product life cycle analysis
5. Appendix
   a. Potential risks
   b. Cost analysis
   c. Technical notes

There are three informational pages. The *title page* displays the formal name of the project; an informal subtitle that explains the formal title (official titles are notoriously uncommunicative); the original issue date, revision number and date, and the geographical location, if important; the names of the authors; and the name of the organization or department. Any document intended for outside use must have a complete mailing address. The version number and its corresponding revision date tell the reader immediately whether the document is current. Imagine the frustration a busy professional feels on discovering that six hours have been spent reading an obsolete document!

The second page contains *sign-offs* by the appropriate managers, users, technical experts, or customers. Many potentially embarrassing misunderstandings are prevented when the system design document itself has spaces for approval signatures, which leaves the responsibility for the document squarely in specific hands. The analyst team will also find increased cooperation from various individuals and their departments when their names are on the approval page. In some situations, the approval list begins with the name of the most senior person. In other cases, the first name listed is that of the user or manager who is ultimately responsible for the system operation. Sensitive analysts consult their own managers to understand the political environment before creating the approval list, which helps prevent ego problems. The approval-page format is another example of logical documentation techniques forcing good management procedures.

The *change-control page* lists all important changes that have taken place since the last release of the document. If, for example, the accounting manager has studied the initial design and found seven unacceptable recommendations, the change control page can be reviewed to determine whether the objections have been resolved. The analyst must never force a busy reader to search through a seventy-five-page document merely to discover what items have changed—the author can save the readers valuable time by using the change-control approach.

One note of caution: analysts under extreme pressure from management to finalize a design project may be tempted to sneak in changes they know should be highlighted through the change-control page technique. The basic concept of change control assumes trust between the author and the reading audience, and even one violation will destroy the author's credibility. Other members of the project team could then see a carefully nurtured attitude of positive cooperation replaced by a wary and distrustful user base. The penalty for dishonesty in technical writing is both immediate and severe.

The following example illustrates the first three pages of a business-oriented systems design document.

Title Page

WORM FARM MANAGEMENT SYSTEM

A new online interactive application system to manage the accounting functions of Dirt Enterprises, a subsidiary of Wonderful Widgets, Inc.

by Karen Keystroke
Systems Analyst
Dirt Enterprises
Muddy Flats, Iowa
July 1, 1985

This document is: Version 3
Issue date: September 4, 1985

Second Page

Changes since version 2 (August 15, 1985): All changes in the text have been flagged with an *x* in the left-hand margin.

1. Discarded plan to band all worms with an ID tag. We will band only adult worms (online volume cut in half).

2. Added three extra month-end reports.

3. A worm accidentally sliced in pieces will be tracked by separate data-base records linked to the original worm as the parent. Only three such choppings will be tracked.

4. Created separate worm history data base for outstanding reproducers.

Third Page

This document must be approved by the following people:

	Signature	Date
Herman Dirt President, Dirt Enterprises	_____	____
Gary Grimy Production Manager	_____	____
Carl Crawly MIS Manager	_____	____
Terrance Tightwad III Controller	_____	____

The *summary* encapsulates the entire design, highlighting the most important features and providing the reader with a good overview. As with the business plan, many casual readers will study only the summary, and the author should write the summary with great care. Many times the analyst can copy the summary from the requirements document or business plan, with just a few minor changes. In technical writing, borrowing from one document to feed another is perfectly acceptable—in fact, such copying is an excellent idea!

In the course of any design process, the analyst team members create a set of *assumptions and guidelines* in their conversations and debates. These assumptions may even dictate the system design choices. Unless the author understands that virtually all departments have unwritten policies that drive the direction of various projects and activities, specifying these policies on paper will be awkward. Some experienced analysts claim it is more difficult to define these assumptions than to create the design itself! Organizations themselves usually function through a set of policies, guidelines, helpful hints, customs, and personal preferences of senior managers. This is often described as the companies' "style," and it definitely affects the entire design process.

Even a moderately complex system design requires a separate unit that presents the *system flow* from both a user and a technical viewpoint. That is, the reader must understand the mechanics of the application in terms of user input, the computer processing, and the output. Although graphs and charts are ideal ways of communicating, one easy-to-use textual method is the *user-computer timing chart,* which describes the logical sequence of events. This approach uses a page split down the middle. The column on the left is labeled "User" (or is given a more specific title) and the right-hand column is labeled "Computer." Normally, action 1 is in the User column, and action 2, in the Computer column, is the corresponding computer processing. Action 3 may then be another user response. In complex environments, the user may perform several actions before the computer performs any actions. A side-by-side timing chart is an excellent way to visualize person-machine interfaces.

These user-computer timing charts are essential when the system design requires specific human responses or activities as a prelude to computer processing. To understand an online receiving system in a warehouse, for example, readers of the document should review several important manual activities that must be performed before, during, and after the computer actions. Unless the development team and the user representatives have a common understanding of the timing involved in human-machine interactions, the company risks serious problems during the development and implementation phases. *A business system usually involves people as well as computers.* A design document that concentrates only on the MIS aspects of a new system or major modification is confusing, frustrating, and incomplete at best. At worst, it could literally destroy the project.

The formats of the *inputs, processing logic,* and *output* sections of the system design document depend on the needs of the project and the experience of the analyst team. Some technical writers copy the style of previous design documents, whereas others choose the format that has served them successfully in the past.

The *inputs* section describes such functions as transactions, completed forms, data collection, and information from other application systems. A comprehensive input section describes every user, computer, and machine interface with the system in terms of both user understanding and MIS implementation. Since users will probably study the input section more than any other portion of the document, the analyst should carefully present the input side of the design in user terminology rather than technical jargon.

Processing is more complicated to explain, because the author must link together information from the input side of the system with the actual computer manipulations. The author must also understand that the processing logic will not function in a complete vacuum. Very rarely will any system design propose a completely stand-alone system that has no relationship to a current data base or information file. In many cases, a proposed system uses some current information, facts, processing, logic, or data from existing files. The author should define the processing to the extent that a programmer/analyst can immediately understand the basic logic requirements. The programmer/analyst may not comprehend enough details to create a program flowchart, but the processing section in any design document should provide a firm starting point. When there is any confusion about the technical requirements, the author must ask for assistance. The ultimate readers of the processing section will be glad to help—after all, they depend on the system design document and especially the processing section for their success.

The following is a simple example of a user-computer timing chart:

RECEIVING DEPARTMENT	WORM FARM MANAGEMENT SYSTEM
1. Truck pulls up to dock with shipment of worms. Clerk enters PO number from driver's bill of lading.	
	2. System verifies open PO number and displays vendor, expected number of cases, and due-in date.
3. Clerk counts number of cases and compares to bill of lading. If there is any problem, clerk notifies Purchasing. If there is a match, clerk enters receipt transaction.	
	4. System marks PO as "received," adds it to overnight AP batch log, and sends online notification to Worm Quality Control (WQC).
5. Clerk removes five worms at random and verifies color, length, and weight. If worms within standards, clerk enters level 1 QA acceptance.	
	6. System prints an inspection report on receiving dock with vendor quality history information.
7. Clerk sends inspection report and bill of lading to Worm Inventory Control (WIC).	

The *outputs* section is easier to write. Analysts describe such visual output as CRT screens or hard-copy reports. Systems with a report generator require a list of data elements available to the user along with sample reports. If a query or "ad hoc" language is used, the author should give several examples. A project that contains user-oriented fourth-generation languages still requires an output section, although the analyst team may provide examples and procedures rather than detailed output formats.

Error conditions are often neglected, because the author generally includes them randomly throughout the document. Whereas various error conditions and their resolutions should indeed be mentioned in each section or chapter, larger system designs dealing with complex application systems need a separate section that discusses only problem resolution. Things do go wrong occasionally! Readers often play devil's advocate and consider the effects of incorrect transactions, computer unavailability, and other assorted disasters. What happens if a general-ledger chart of accounts error occurs in an accounts payable transaction? What is the correction procedure? How does the system respond? When must it be corrected? The answers may be scattered throughout the document, but concerned users (and equally concerned MIS professionals) feel more comfortable when they discover all the answers to these disconcerting questions in one place.

The *hardware, software, and personnel requirements* section contains the resources necessary for both development and continued operation of the system. Most installations have standard formats used in budget-planning documents that can be successfully copied in the systems design paper. If such a format is not available, the author can simply state the requirements in a line-by-line arrangement.

If the proposed system will *interface* with any existing application, data base, process, or machine, the system design document should identify and discuss each interface. Some analysts mention each interface point briefly and allow the staff to investigate the details in the development phase. Others spend considerable time researching the problems caused by an interface. Both approaches are valid as long as the authors and their managers understand the choice.

The *appendix* is a collection of valuable information that does not fit into any mainline section. In general, these facts tend to be specific to one group or person and are not applicable to a wider audience. If material applies to several people or a group, the author should use it in the main sections. If, however, the information appeals to only one person or is so technical that most readers would immediately turn the page, it belongs in the appendix. The author of a system design document without an appendix may be in trouble! Either everything has been stuffed in the main body or facts that are important to certain individuals have been omitted. Whatever the reason, the MIS director should be prepared for future problems. An appendix may not look impressive, but it definitely serves a useful purpose.

3.7 THE COST-BENEFITS ANALYSIS

After the system design has been approved, one important step remains before the project can receive final approval. Management must now answer the ultimate question: Is it worth the effort and cost? The vehicle for solving the puzzle is a *cost-benefits analysis* that compares development and operating cost to the tangible and intangible benefits. If the comparison is favorable, the project should continue. If not, logic dictates that the proposal be modified or even scrapped. Although some analysts attempt a cost-benefits analysis even before the system has been designed, the value of such an exercise is limited. Only the system design will tell management the true cost of the project, and only after the analysis and design effort are completed will the project team and users understand the true value of a new application.

The term "intangible benefits" frightens not only many technical writers, but the most fearless management team. It mystifies so many people that some organizations skip the cost-benefits analysis and make the ultimate decision by default. *Tangible* benefits, of course, are easy to calculate, and senior managers expect some justification. But most organizations fail to make the cost-benefits analysis part of the normal project review procedure. Should a specific project be implemented? In some situations, if no one objects, the project is put on the pending list, and if the senior vice president thinks the concept is an excellent idea, the project will be given top priority. The lack of a cost-benefits analysis for major projects is a form of "management by crisis," "management by default," or even "management by squeaky wheel." Good management policy requires that all major projects include a cost-benefits analysis after the system design phase. Managers who claim they can make logical business decisions without a cost-benefits analysis usually make second- or even third-rate decisions.

The format of a cost-benefits analysis is simple: section A contains the estimated development and ongoing costs, and section B describes the benefits and makes the final recommendation. The entire document is rarely over two or three pages long. Experienced analysts add a final paragraph that gives a *level of confidence* concerning all the costs and benefits in the document. A high level of confidence suggests that management can trust the analysis and its conclusion, whereas a low level of confidence (with appropriate reasons) makes management's job more difficult. It is a fact of life in the world of information systems that some estimates are better than others, and the organization that understands this reality can make more accurate business decisions.

Developmental costs are usually estimated separately for programming design, programming, testing, documentation, and implementation. Whereas there are many accepted ways to display such estimates, a simple method that can be easily explained is the concept of *calendar weeks*. That is, estimating a task at six calendar weeks means that an experienced programmer would complete that assignment in six weeks if assigned to that job full-time. This estimate takes into account normal administrative time (usually 20 percent), but it does not consider multiple assignments, vacations, or illnesses. It also assumes an experienced programmer or analyst, not one who needs specialized training. The calendar week concept is still a useful tool for roughly estimating development projects and can later be converted to precise worker-day estimates when the programming specifications are complete. For planning purposes, MIS managers can then factor in the degree of experience of likely candidates, the probability of multiple assignments, and other risks.

Ongoing costs are difficult to estimate, because companies have various ways of computing charge-back costs, ranging from the very accurate to the very ridiculous. One might argue that an in-house computer that has excess capacity is actually "free" for additional batch applications (other than incidental materials, such as tapes and disk packs). The operations manager, struggling to justify a budget, would naturally disagree, whereas the company president might agree in principle, since it will not increase the expense line on the profit-and-loss statement. Even if the requesting department is charged according to some proven resource unit–type accounting method, how much does the new system actually cost to run? Which cost should be used in a cost-benefits analysis? Systems analysts, user managers, and MIS directors have spent many frustrating hours pondering that problem, but the obvious solution is to use *both* costs. Or, if there are three reasonable ways to view the operating costs of a new system or application, the technical writer should list *all three*! For example, a valid ongoing cost estimate charged to the requesting department could be listed as $5,000 per month for "computer time" or as a much lower $100 per month for increased material expenses. Both are "correct," and management should see both sides of the costing issue.

Hardware purchases can be more complicated, because the changing tax laws permit purchases to be charged in various ways that can affect the cost-benefits analysis. Can these ten additional CRTs be amortized over five years if they are purchased? What about leasing them and using the capital for another purpose? An accountant familiar with the business side of data processing can make suggestions pertaining to the accounting, depreciation, and tax liability considerations. The author of a cost-benefits analysis should never simply report raw numbers when it comes to hardware. Instead, the author should work with an accountant and present several scenarios that will have different financial effects.

On a more basic level, however, many MIS directors complain that systems analysts not familiar with computer hardware consistently underestimate the final cost of new hardware and its supporting equipment. A classic example is the case of an expensive minicomputer, disk drive, and printer sitting idle because the systems analyst forgot to check the power requirements and the units cannot be plugged in until the electricians install new wiring even more expensive than the hardware! Slight omissions can be disastrous when trying to estimate costs.

The benefits section should include both the tangible and intangible benefits and answer the question: Why should we spend *x* number of dollars doing this project? Tangible benefits are those that can be measured in terms of dollars saved or time gained, whereas intangible benefits are those hard-to-quantify advantages that will increase productivity, improve quality, or provide better information for management decisions. If the author has a choice, it is best to concentrate on the measurable benefits, such as manpower savings (reduction in number or possible reassignment of staff members), lower operating expenses, future cost avoidance, or a greater opportunity for using financial resources. But as data processing grabs up more and more of the routine production jobs, it becomes more difficult to show direct cost benefits, and systems analysts must use their ingenuity to explain those intangible but important benefits. Just how much better is online journal entry editing than batch editing? Will productivity increase significantly? How much is online processing worth to the organization and its bottom line?

There are no easy answers to such complex questions,

and experienced analysts have found no standard way to explain intangible benefits. One obvious method is to carefully paraphrase the explanations of those in the company who have a strong opinion as to the value of the project. Although the originator of the concept may be prejudiced in favor of his own idea, he may still have the best mental picture of the intangible benefits to be derived. The systems analyst should always work with the user in documenting these improvements or advantages, although some human perceptions tend to be more emotional than factual. Accounting manager Lana Ledger may laugh and say, "Of course we need online editing. Any fool can see that." With a little encouragement and the right probing questions from the analyst, Lana may be able to provide a few subjective but nonetheless impressive reasons for considering online editing a valid company objective.

Even if the cost and benefits sections are accurate, the conclusion section may be relatively complicated. The systems analyst who writes the cost-benefits analysis may be emotionally involved with the concept (because of the amount of time spent on the project) and may be unaware of the current MIS situation. But it is essential for the author to provide some recommendation even if the author does not understand the full ramifications of the final decision. The systems analyst may not have any input into the final decision-making process, but the analyst bears the responsibility for weighing the cost against the tangible and intangible benefits and making the best value judgment possible.

3.8 PROGRAMMING SPECIFICATIONS

After the project has been approved, the technical staff must prepare the detailed program specifications. Although some new fourth-generation languages are indeed moving away from this classic stage of application development by generating their own *source code*, third-generation languages such as COBOL and PL/I will be around for a long time. For third-generation applications, the analyst team must create high-quality programming specifications that will allow the programming staff to develop a system that will successfully match the system design.

Some managers are tempted to slight or even skip the program specification stage, especially when the same staff members who created the system design will do the detailed programming. This is dangerous because of the primitive nature of third-generation languages. The logic and detailed coding are often too complicated for even a good programmer to take a system design and create the individual program modules. Although a few rare design documents do have enough specific detail to be used as programming documentation, most experts feel that systems built with any third-generation language still need specifically tailored documentation that can be easily transferred into source code. This may be called *pseudocode* or *high-level code* and is the necessary link between design and coding.

The degree of detail in programming specifications depends on the complexity of the modules, the skills of the technical staff members, and their familiarity with the application. If the project involves extensive changes to an existing system and the programmer must make complex logic changes, the programming specifications should describe not only the changes but the important existing processing as well. Even if the new requirements are spelled out in great detail, the new module may fail if the programmer did not understand how the changes interface with the existing logic. It is better to include too much rather than too little!

The nature of programming specifications also depends on the management policy concerning technical documentation in general. Does the organization have any program-level documentation in place? If so, can the programmer/analyst use that same format in creating new programming specifications? Professionals should try for consistency even if the existing formats are not totally acceptable, because *the programming specifications of today should become the maintenance documentation of tomorrow*. Therefore, the programmer/analyst should keep one eye on present needs and the other eye on future applications. The programmer may get a splitting headache, but this double emphasis encourages the efficient use of company resources. Documentation is a company resource just as much as a building, a computer, or a stamping machine. Programming specifications should be easy to change, and the programmer/analyst should avoid the typewriter for the same reason the analyst should avoid the typewriter; a word processor should be used for programming specifications. In fact, program-level documentation may be changed more frequently than many design documents. As new programmers learn about a module or make extensive changes, they may be willing to update the program-level documentation under three conditions: (1) if the supervisor encourages the practice, (2) if they are given adequate time, and (3) if the process is relatively easy.

Programmers avoid written documentation if they must go through the hassle of having pages retyped. The ideal medium for any program-level documentation is an online system that interfaces with a word-processing package and allows the computer to handle the mechnical problems of formatting the output.

There are many styles of program-level specifications (under several names), but two of the more common "generic" approaches are the input-processing-output (IPO) and module-to-module (MTM) approaches. Some programmers use a combination of these two classical approaches. Known by many names, described by numerous authors, and existing in multiple variations, these two approaches are the basic foundations of many existing documentation schemes. Indeed, advocates of certain programming practices insist that program design specifications follow their own brand of documentation. The structured programming adherents, for example, have definite ideas about detailed programming documentation that have proved successful in a number of situations. But it is unwise to assume that all environments, organizations, and projects should always follow one specific format unless management has made a conscious decision to follow one particular design methodology. The purpose of mentioning the IPO and MTM approaches is simply to present useful examples that may or may not fit a particular project.

The IPO technique is an older method that analyzes a program in terms of data and files coming in, the processing that must be applied, and the output, such as reports, record streams, CRT screens, messages, and data files. This style can apply equally well to both online and batch programs and can be adapted to data-base or telecommunications environments.

The MTM method is appropriate when a program or system consists of many separately compiled modules, each of which has its own particular function, such as input, processing, or output. Each module has a specific purpose with one entry and exit point, and the true complexity —from a programming viewpoint—is relating each module to the main calling routine. The module-to-module approach is useful when the programmer anticipates major logic changes in the system once it is in production.

Both of these approaches will be discussed in Chapter 9.

3.9 THE CHRONO FILE

History is fascinating. When the inevitable questions arise after a project is complete, analysts and managers scratch their collective heads and ask, "What exactly happened? When did it happen?" It is better if the purpose is not so much to fix blame as to answer valid questions and help the organization learn from the past. Project management systems generally do not supply the answer, although they do track detailed project schedules.

The chrono file should be kept by the project leader or section manager and should begin at the feasibility stage. Too often, MIS management fails to realize that even blue-sky discussions with users are truly part of the project development cycle and should rightly be charged to that activity. If a project leader has not been assigned during the feasibility stage, the systems analyst should start the file by logging in any facts related to the timing and individual accomplishments, even if they are nothing more than one-line notations.

Useful information in a chrono file might be:

- When did the design phase start?
- Who did the initial write-up?
- How much time was spent on it?
- How much user involvement did it require?
- Who approved the design, and who provided internal communication?
- How long did the approval process take?
- Who requested changes to the design, and how long did each change take?
- Did the change require a full reevaluation of the project?
- Who gave the first cost estimates and when? How far off were they?

If the project leader keeps the chrono file continually updated, at the end of a development project it will be an extremely valuable historic document tracing the key events of the entire project. Although other formal reporting procedures can be helpful, a manager who wants to analyze project history should utilize the chrono file as a document designed specifically for that purpose.

3.10 SUMMARY OF KEY POINTS

☐ Good documentation practices can solve many project management problems; conversely, many problems in project development are caused by poor documents.

☐ The proposal should be written by both users and MIS.

☐ The proposal document should include justification—why is the idea important?

☐ The proposal package needs a cover letter and an appendix.

☐ The feasibility study may be the most forgotten document in MIS, yet it forces MIS management to take an early position "on the record." Is the project feasible? This document will often save wasted unproductive effort.

☐ Both business and technical factors are important in the feasibility study.

☐ If the MIS analyst cannot recommend a course of action, the feasibility study must include suggestions on the next step in the evaluation process.

☐ Business plans are important for all large projects and for small projects that are complex or have a high-risk factor. The business plan is a road map that tells MIS where to go and how to get there. It is a procedural, management-oriented document.

☐ Every requirements document should explicitly state the level of detail and why it was chosen. The readers must know whether the requirements are complete or only a starting point.

☐ Each requirement should be labeled as either absolute, recommended, or optional. A document that merely lists requirements without comparing their relative importance may cause problems later in the development cycle.

☐ System design documents are a reference tool. They must be easy to change and written in the stand-alone mode.

☐ For system designs, both graphics and text should be used to communicate effectively.

☐ There is no single format that is best for all system design documents. The analyst's or technical writer's work should be customized to fit the situation.

☐ System designs should always list the assumptions and guidelines used by the analyst team.

☐ The writer should emphasize error handling and error recovery procedures—people want to know what happens when things go wrong.

☐ The cost-benefits analysis tells management whether the project is worth doing. This analysis is made after the system design is completed and before programming begins. It is a final check on feasibility that prevents major disasters.

☐ The programming specifications for a new project should eventually become maintenance documentation.

chapter *4*

Internal MIS Forms

INTRODUCTION

This chapter shows how to create and use service requests; project status reports; task control forms; weekly, monthly, and quarterly status reports; experience evaluation forms; and memos. Without efficient and effective internal forms and reports, an MIS department may flounder in a sea of miscommunication. Well-designed forms are an extension of a sound management program; every aspect of each form serves a specific purpose. MIS managers and senior professional staff members can use these ready-to-copy examples (with instructions) to revitalize their internal communication.

MIS paperwork should be viewed as an *opportunity*, because various forms and reports *can actually help implement management direction.* In effect, they *become* the management policy, and the difference between a well-run organization and one that merely stumbles along is often the quality of its internal paperwork. If the paperwork situation is a nightmare, the rest of the department may be equally frightening.

Reports and forms must be standardized for the same reasons that companies standardize programming languages. A shop that allowed every programmer to choose a unique language would be a disaster, and in a slightly less dramatic way a department that allowed every staff member to choose a unique reporting or documentation format would be equally unorganized. Standards are implemented because they will "pay off" in terms of more efficient communication and greater productivity. Standards are there to help communication rather than hinder it.

Although it is not possible to cover the complex subject of forms design in this text, managers who implement standardized forms for their departments must always consider human psychology. For example, if a particular form provides a relatively large amount of space for a specific question, the respondent will feel encouraged to fill the space. A very large section labeled "problems" suggests that the respondent should conjure up a significant amount of written explanation. A smaller space for a section labeled "any other matters to report?" will discourage a response. People normally attempt to complete a questionnaire in a manner that will please the originator. The forms designer or manager should always try forms and report formats on perceptive volunteers who can point out such subtle but important factors.

4.1 SERVICE REQUESTS

A good service request form must be complete enough to identify the request and its disposition but relatively easy for all to understand. The form becomes a working document that enables MIS management to track the request, its eventual completion, and its effect on other systems, applications, and departments. The service request form then becomes a permanent historical document as part of a formal auditing system. It may even be subject to legal retention requirements, as in some industries that deal with the Food and Drug Administration, the Environmental Protection Agency, or the Department of Defense.

4.1.1 Identifying Service Requests

The basis of every service request is the identification scheme to track and log requests from both the users and internal staff members. Obviously, each request must have some identification (ID) number or tag, but a simple sequential numbering scheme is inefficient. "Request number 76543" tells nothing significant about the request, except that it was made after 76542 and before 76544. Since each request must be identified anyway, it is logical to develop a scheme that conveys some information about the nature of the request. There are many ways to create meaningful identification systems, and it is possible to develop horrendously complicated schemes that look great on paper but fail miserably when put into practice.

A simple but effective method uses the following format:

YY-SS-0001-T

where YY is the last two digits of the year, SS is the two-digit or two-character mnemonic for the application system involved, 0001 is the sequential number, and T is the type of request.

As a result of using the year as the first segment of the ID number, requests can be logged in chronological sequence and retrieved according to date, although date of submission varies in importance from installation to installation.

The purpose of having a two-position system identification is to break down requests according to the nature of the application or production system. Many shops are organized into support teams, or at least have individual programmers assigned to groups of specific applications. A request ID number that has a PY for Payroll or an AP for Accounts Payable immediately identifies the responsible area or department.

Once assigned to a request, the ID number will not change, except for the type code. In many business data-processing organizations, a request to investigate a problem or condition may subsequently cause the originator to ask for a programming change. The original form can be used by simply changing the type code to indicate a system change rather than a research investigation.

The basic type codes are:

I: Investigation

P: Reported problem that needs research

A: Serious problem that needs immediate research

D: Data modification

F: File or database error

C: Application system change

H: Assistance needed from programming

J: Special job needed

R: Rerun needed

M: Miscellaneous request

A few of the countless variations on this identification format are:

- Using the calendar month instead of the year, if chronological order is extremely important.
- Using the year and calendar month (YYMM).
- Replacing the two-position application mnemonic with the two- or three-position name of the requesting unit, as with ACC for accounting, FIN for finance, and MER for merchandising.
- Replacing the two-position application mnemonic with a code for the name of the analyst or manager taking the request.

- Adding a priority code as the first digit of the sequential number, where 1 could indicate the lowest and 5 the highest priority. However, since priority in some companies can change as often as the phases of the moon, this apparently logical approach can be confusing.

Each installation should create its own ID scheme that will allow a staff member to immediately categorize most requests. The format should not be too cumbersome, for people will hesitate to use it, but neither should it be a simple sequential number that tells nothing. The ID scheme should at least answer the three basic questions of who, where, and when.

A standard format for a service request form is shown in Figure 4.1a.

4.1.2 Writing Instructions for Users

Most forms need accompanying instructions. Some employees consistently have trouble completing certain forms and reports even when the author of the document believes the masterpiece can be filled out by any intelligent second grader. It is the responsibility of the author and management to verify that most forms are designed not only to follow management policy but to consider human engineering. Employees often need instructions either embedded in the form or in a separate document.

The set of instructions in Figure 4.1b applies to the MIS service request shown in Figure 4.1a.

4.1.3 Tracking and Managing Service Requests

For most MIS service request forms, the back of the form is the ideal space for tracking the status, condition, and eventual disposition of the request on the front side. For some strange reason, many technical writers refuse to use both sides of a form, even if they must create another document. Figure 4.2 illustrates a format for tracking requests.

FORM DP-1

Wonderful Widgets, Inc.
Management Information Systems Division
SERVICE REQUEST

Please fill out section A, except for the two entries labeled "For MIS Use Only."
If you have any questions, please see Form DP-1.
Thanks for your cooperation.

SECTION A

Date: _____

Submitted by: _____

Department: _____

Phone: _____

Office number: _____

Requested priority:

Emergency ____   As time permits ____

Immediate ____   Time critical   ____

Normal   ____

For MIS Use Only

Log number:____ - ____ - _____

Rec'd by: _____

When do you need it done? _____

Application system: _____

Figure 4.1a Service Request Form

Do you want to be notified by phone when
this request is done? _____

Do you want to talk about this request in person? _____

Description of request: _____

_____

_____

_____

_____

_____

_____

Thank you. This ends section A.

SECTION B: FOR MIS USE ONLY

Evaluated by: _____

Date received: _____   Time received: _____

Type (if the type changes, cross out the old classifica-
tion):

Serious problem that needs immediate
attention   A ____

Problem that needs research   P ____

Application system change   C ____

Data modification   D ____

Assistance needed from Programming   H ____

Investigation   I ____

Special job needed   J ____

Figure 4.1a *(Continued)*

Miscellaneous request   M ____

Rerun needed   R ____

Initial priority: 1   2   3   4   5   Date _____

Second priority: 1   2   3   4   5   Date _____

Third priority: 1   2   3   4   5   Date _____

Disposition: _____

Applications involved: _____
_____

Route to other groups: _____

Date routed: _____   Routed to: _____
_____
_____

Estimated completion date: _____

Follow-up requirements: _____
_____
_____

Comments: _____
_____
_____
_____
_____
_____
_____

Figure 4.1a   Service Request Form (*Continued*)

The purpose of this form is to help MIS serve you better. The more accurate the information, the better we can serve your needs. DP-1 is easy to use—just follow the instructions for each line.

Date: Use today's date in month, day, year format.

Submitted by: Your first and last name.

Requesting department: Use the formal department name followed by your section or group name.

Submitter's phone and office number: Use your extension and office number. If you are located in the office annex, put an "A" after your office number.

Priority requested: How critical is this request? Use the "emergency" code only if it is a serious production problem or if the request must be completed ASAP. Use the "immediate" code only if the request has a deadline within 72 hours. Use the "normal" code most of the time. If the request has a low priority, check "as time permits." If you check "normal" but the request must be done by a certain time, check "time critical."

Log number: Do not fill in!

Received by: Do not fill in!

When do you need it done? If there is a time requirement, list it here. Use this line only if the requirement is important.

Application system(s): If you know the specific applications involved, list them on this line. If you are not sure, leave it blank.

Do you want to be notified by phone when request is done? Check "yes" if you want to be called. (We always send a copy of the completed request form.)

Do you want to talk about this request in person? Check "yes" if you need a meeting to discuss the request or the timing. We will then contact you.

Description of request: Please describe what you need.

Figure 4.1*b* Instructions for Service Request Form

Use extra pages if necessary. Attach any other paperwork that provides information. Try to be complete, but don't worry about MIS jargon.

If you are not sure which MIS department needs to review your request, send this form to MIS Control (office 407-B). However, if you are reasonably certain which MIS group will handle your request, send the form to that group in care of the production services coordinator. Be sure to keep a copy for yourself.

The MIS control clerk, the production services coordinator, or the unit manager will send you a copy with a tentative completion date in the upper right-hand corner. Next to the estimated completion date will be the MIS priority code, with 5 the highest and 1 the lowest priority. If you do not agree with either the date or the priority, please call the unit manager.

We may contact you for additional information. We always try to be as accurate as possible, and sometimes we have questions that must be answered before we can give you an estimated completion date.

When your request has been completed, MIS will send you another copy of the completed request. If you have asked to be notified by phone when the request is completed, the MIS control clerk will call you or leave a message with your department secretary.

If you have any questions about the form, your request, or its current status, please contact MIS Control at extension 4598, or call the unit production services coordinator.

Thank you.

Figure 4.1b Instructions for Service Request Form (*Continued*)

Log number: ____ - ____ - ____

FOR MIS USE ONLY

Date assigned: _____   Assigned to: _____

Instructions: _____

_____

_____

Estimated completion date: _____

Time critical? _____   For more info., see: _____

Completion date: _____   Filed by: _____

User notified on: _____   Notified by: _____

Date assigned: _____   Assigned to: _____

Instructions: _____

_____

_____

Estimated completion date: _____

Time critical: _____   For more info., see: _____

Completion date: _____   Filed by: _____

User notified on: _____   Notified by: _____

_____

_____

_____

Figure 4.2 Back of the Service Request Form

The back of the form should hold at least two repetitions of this information, because some requests are moved from person to person as the assignment becomes more difficult or the priorities change. The coordinator can easily attach additional request forms and use only the back to track the request as it is moved to a third or even a fourth person. Requests even move from department to department—for instance, from Programming to Data Control to Operations.

Whereas forms are traditionally oriented toward hard copy, a shop with a plentiful supply of CRTs should consider putting request forms online—if the majority of users have access to a CRT. However, if most requests come with attached paperwork, such as flowcharts, memos, report samples, or formulas, it is more efficient to use hard-copy request forms. Paper may seem old-fashioned to those who dabble in online, interactive processing, but it still can be an effective medium for communication.

The proper management of service requests is a complex topic with its own rules and procedures, most of which vary from organization to organization. The most effective rules for controlling request forms are:

1. Process all requests within four business days. The user should receive a copy with the MIS portion filled out, or at least an explanation for any delay. Even if it will take six months or six years to complete a request, the user should be informed that MIS has reviewed the idea. This "four business day" requirement is an excellent way to demonstrate a businesslike attitude. People respond favorably when MIS shows a sense of professionalism.

2. Keep only one copy of the request in MIS. Duplicate copies of the request may cause the same problem as duplicate data: it is hard to keep them current. Even at the risk of losing an occasional request, the analyst or programmer handling the assignment should keep the only MIS copy. Of course, if the request is entered into an online tracking system, that material will never be lost unless the system crashes and erases the data.

3. Request forms must always have current status information. Some analysts and programmers dislike record keeping so much they become careless and forget to update the form as work progresses. Such employees rely only on their memories. This is a poor business practice that encourages misunderstanding and confusion.

    4. When the task is complete, notify the user. Never assume that the person who makes the request will magically know that the task or special computer run has been completed. Few users are highly proficient in mind reading and ESP. Notifying all users (both internal and external to MIS) is another simple but professional business practice.

The internal tracking device for service requests is the *request log,* which lists all pending requests and their current status. Without an accurate request log, it is virtually impossible to properly manage a large number of work requests. More than three requests is usually considered a large number.

A sample format is shown in Figure 4.3, but hard-copy logs are both cumbersome and inefficient. Logs work best when stored on a computerized text editor or word-processing system.

4.2 PROJECT REPORTING

Project management is a fascinating subject, with many books available on methods, procedures, and case histories. The trade press is filled with advertisements and discussions of various project management systems and related software. But almost all project management methodologies depend on a written document to communicate their status. Interestingly enough, even very different project management approaches may have similar reporting requirements. In general, the readers of any project management report need answers to six basic questions:

    1. How is the project coming?
    2. How much progress has been made since the last report?
    3. What major checkpoints have been reached?
    4. What is the next major checkpoint?

FORM DP-2

Wonderful Widgets, Inc.
Management Information Systems
SERVICE REQUEST CONTROL LOG

Status codes: I (in evaluation), H (hold), W (in progress), C (complete), A (assigned but not started), X (complete and user notified)

LOG	DESCRIPTION	DATE REC'D	PRIORITY	ASSIGNED To	ASSIGNED Date	TYPE	STATUS	DATE COMPLETED

Figure 4.3 Service Request Control Log

5. Are there any major problems the readers should know about?
6. Are you on schedule? If not, why not?

The difference between a good project control form and a poor one is not necessarily the volume of information, but the efficiency of communication. How well does the form convey information? Good project control forms are not only easier to use, but *actually force professionals to accurately evaluate their true status.* After completing the form, the employee should know without a doubt how his or her position relates to the project schedule.

Whatever the format, standardized project control forms and procedures help the staff become familiar with only one set of requirements. Project managers should seldom be allowed to experiment with reporting formats if the shop has working standards. Experimentation is often justified in some aspects of data processing, but project management is too important to be left to a manager's whim. Rather, management as a group should select a format and associated procedures that satisfy the requirements and should not change this format unless someone clearly demonstrates a better tool.

Of course, every form in the civilized world will eventually change as managers and employees gain experience with its strong and weak points. This change should be approached cautiously, but the organization should never be afraid to strive for improvement.

4.2.1 Characteristics of Project Control Forms

Any good, flexible, and practical project control form should meet these seven basic requirements:

1. It should be easy for the professional to fill out and should not require the employee to spend more time on the report than on the actual project.
2. It should allow the staff member to provide information by simply circling a description or making a checkmark

rather than writing words or phrases. Most project management answers can be anticipated by the designer of the form, so it is relatively easy for the author to create a format that reduces unnecessary writing.

3. It should not use complicated project management jargon. If a form contains vocabulary that can only be understood by staff members who have read the latest thirty books on project management theory, the form will handicap employees rather than help them.

4. It should have free space to allow the employees to enter additional information that does not readily fit into the general framework of a formatted report.

5. It should be positive in tone. Project control forms that stress the "problem" aspect of data processing can be depressing. Problems, complaints, and frustrations are common to data processing, but a form that has the heading "List Problems Here" in overwhelming large, red letters encourages people to focus on the negative aspects. Rather, the titles and sections should emphasize the progress made instead of the problems encountered. The author should even avoid using the word "problems," if at all possible, since other words such as "difficulties" and "roadblocks" convey the same meaning without the negative connotation.

6. It should be prepared in a professional manner. The form should not simply be typed by the secretary and then photocopied. A better approach is to have it professionally printed, which will help the employees see the project control form as an important document that requires accuracy, thought, and effort. A sloppy or primitive-looking form encourages sloppy or primitive reporting habits.

7. Its format should help individual employees visualize their progress as it relates to the *total project development schedule*. That is, it should allow them to arrange their tasks so that they can see their status in relation to the important project milestones. Such checkpoints should not be limited to the conventional categories of *code, compile,* and *test,* but should use events in time that are meaningful for that particular project and the people who will be using that form.

Figure 4.4 presents a sample project control form that can be used by programmers, programmer/analysts, sys-

FORM DP-3

Wonderful Widgets, Inc.
Management Information Systems Division
PROJECT REPORTING FORM

Name: _____ Dept.: ____

Number: _____ Date: _____

Project name: _____ Project code: ____

Period covered: From _____ to _____

Circle the activities in progress:

  Design   Program specs   Code testing   Interface

  Unit testing   User education   Documentation

  Implementation   Follow-up   Internal documentation

1. List any tasks completed during this reporting period:

TASK	ACTUAL START DATE	ACTUAL END DATE	PLANNED END DATE
_____	_____	_____	_____
_____	_____	_____	_____
_____	_____	_____	_____
_____	_____	_____	_____
_____	_____	_____	_____
_____	_____	_____	_____
_____	_____	_____	_____
_____	_____	_____	_____
_____	_____	_____	_____
_____	_____	_____	_____

Figure 4.4 Project Reporting Form

2. List any tasks or jobs in progress:

TASK	STATUS (% COM- PLETE)	ESTIMATED END DATE
_____	_____	_____
_____	_____	_____
_____	_____	_____
_____	_____	_____

3. List any holdups or stumbling blocks encountered during this reporting period.

_____

_____

_____

4. Do you have any goals for the next reporting period that are not mentioned in question 2?

_____

_____

_____

5. Do you anticipate any difficulties during this next reporting period?

_____

_____

6. According to your current understanding, are you on schedule with your assignments?

_____

_____

Figure 4.4 Project Reporting Form (*Continued*)

7. List the assignments of other project team members or users that could have a critical path impact on your progress during the next two reporting periods.

_____

_____

_____

8. Do you have enough project work to keep busy during the next reporting period?

_____

_____

_____

9. List any significant nonproject work you have performed during this reporting period. Estimate the time spent and the degree of difficulty.

_____

_____

_____

10. Is there anything else your manager should know about your work or the project itself?

_____

_____

_____

_____

_____

11. Would you like a conference with your manager?

Yes _____   No _____

Figure 4.4 (_Continued_)

tems analysts, and technicians who are involved in a typical development or maintenance project.

4.2.2 Instructions for the Project Control Document

Evaluating project control forms is more of an art than a science. Since professionals differ in their quantity and quality of written expression, a manager may find one employee eager to write ten pages every week and another employee who gives yes or no answers to complex questions. A set of instructions along with feedback from the supervisor may help staff members to correctly judge the amount of effort needed to communicate essential information.

The sample project reporting form shown in Figure 4.4 may seem self-explanatory, but some employees are honestly puzzled by certain questions, especially those that allow free-form answers. Only instructions can prevent this frustrating situation!

Figure 4.5 presents sample instructions that can be used for the project reporting form shown in Figure 4.4. A few minor changes could make it applicable to almost any data-processing organization.

4.2.3 Project Reporting and Management Policy

The sample project reporting form is definitely an instrument of management policy, which is strongly implied by the questions. Employees are asked to anticipate problems, which places the burden of prediction where it belongs. They also must categorically state whether they believe themselves to be on schedule. The question on critical path needs will make them aware of timing restrictions. The form asks whether they have enough productive work to keep busy—if they do not, the supervisor will find them some. In other words, the questions place responsibility directly on the staff members. There is no doubt on a week-by-week basis whether a given professional is on schedule,

Wonderful Widgets, Inc.
Management Information System Division
INSTRUCTIONS FOR COMPLETING PROJECT
REPORTING FORM DP-3

Identifying Information
- Fill out your name, department, employee number, and the date (normally a Monday).
- Write the formal project name and code as listed in your *MIS Procedures Manual.*
- For a weekly reporting period, enter last Monday as the "from" date and last Friday as the "to" date. For a monthly report, use the first Monday of the calendar month as the "from" date and the last Friday of the calendar month as the "to" date. Your project manager may give you special dates for monthly reporting.
- Circle the activities that best describe your status. If you are just finishing one and starting another, circle them both. If these terms do not describe your situation, write your own descriptive name.

Status
1. List completed tasks during this reporting period. Use the task name from your project plan. Enter the date completed and the estimated date from the project plan. For "end date," use the date when all follow-up work was finished.
2. Enter all project-related tasks in progress, but do not include production support or other assignments. The "percent complete" should describe where you stand today. Use a percent figure that is a multiple of 10, such as 40 or 50 percent. Enter the date you started the task and the date you expect to finish. The estimated end date does not have to match the project plan end date, but should reflect your current estimate.

Figure 4.5 Instructions for Project Reporting Form DP-3

3. List any holdups or stumbling blocks you have faced during the past week (or month, if you are on monthly reporting). These can be unexpected design problems, changes in specifications, test time limitations, etc.

4. Define your goals for this week (or month) for the project. Do not repeat any listed in response to question 2.

5. List any anticipated difficulties during this next week (or month).

6. Are you on schedule according to the current project plan? If not, list any reasons that help explain the situation. You may refer to questions 3 and 5, but do not repeat information unless absolutely necessary.

7. List the assignments of other project team members that could hold you up if those tasks are not complete. Use your copy of the master project plan and look at critical path junctions for the next two reporting periods. Write the task number and name.

8. Do you have enough productive work to keep busy? This refers only to project work. If the answer is no, your manager will contact you.

9. List all nonproject work (but not administrative or reporting duties) that have affected your performance. Mention only assignments that were not budgeted in your project plan. For example, include production support tasks only if they went beyond the time originally allocated.

10. Describe anything else your project manager should know about this past week (or month) or about your general progress.

11. Do you wish to meet with your project manager to discuss either this report or the project itself? Check yes or no.

Figure 4.5   Instructions for Form DP-3 (*Continued*)

faces critical path delays, or has enough work to do. *This form helps implement a management policy of "no surprises."*

4.3 TASK CONTROL

First- and second-level managers consistently find that a few programmers, programmer/analysts, and systems analysts seem to accomplish several times more than others in the department. They are commonly described as "good workers" or "highly motivated." But perhaps one reason for the startling difference in performance is that the professionals know how to manage their time, whereas the amateurs let their time manage them. Self-motivation is also an important factor, but even the most highly motivated employees cannot function at full productivity unless they are in control of their tasks, assignments, and daily schedules.

The human mind is notoriously poor at monitoring multiple tasks and schedules at the same time. Although a few lucky people can correctly juggle many assignments simultaneously, most of us need a written tool that tells us what we are working on, how long it should take, its relative priority, and its relationship to other tasks. Those tools are commonly called *project plans* or *task control forms,* and their purpose is to help the professional use correct planning techniques. Planning is another important key to achieving full productivity.

Task control forms vary with the nature of the position and the type of person involved. Some jobs in MIS—such as that of a systems analyst doing research on local area networks—require very little specific task control. The systems analyst may have general weekly or monthly goals, but day-to-day performance is directed by what is found in reading or contacts with other organizations using local area networks. Other positions—such as that of a programmer/analyst doing production support or that of a manager supervising a project team—entail specific duties, and it is individuals in these types of positions who can benefit most from some type of task control form.

A simple manual approach for employees who have rapidly changing assignments is to create a set of plain 3 × 5 filing cards (one card per task) containing the following information:

Work request number

Task name

System

Source of request

Date of Request

Date due

Estimated hours

Actual hours

Completion date

Follow-up needed

These headings can be arranged in a logical order to fit the needs of the organization. If management decides to use a filing card approach, the format should be standardized across all departments in MIS. This information can also be stored in an online system that will give other people the ability to review assignments and progress. An online method is usually preferable to a card system if employees have ready access to CRTs and if the system is designed for simplicity. One common problem is that managers requesting an online system put in so many bells and whistles that the system becomes cumbersome for the employees, which inevitably means that it will slowly fade into oblivion, much to everyone's relief. Simplicity is more than a virtue when implementing task control procedures! Once the system is installed and the staff has become familiar with its operation and benefits, management can slowly add features to provide additional reporting capabilities.

4.4 THE WEEKLY STATUS REPORT

The weekly status report has become as much of a tradition in MIS circles as empty pizza cartons scattered about the offices of programmers facing an impending deadline. Most staff-level employees fill out a report weekly (or at least monthly), and they usually dislike doing this just as much as their managers dislike reading the reports. The problem is not the concept of weekly reporting, but rather that many weekly status reports are virtually worthless. Of course, everyone involved learns the truth very quickly. Staff members know that the status reports do not truly reflect their week, and the manager discovers that weekly reports are seldom useful for either people or task management. Some first-line supervisors tend to treat the weekly status report as just another paperwork nuisance that must be completed before the real work begins.

How unfortunate for everyone in MIS! The weekly status report provides a perfect opportunity for the employees to show exactly what they have accomplished and where they now stand, and an equally promising opportunity for management to capture the activities of each staff member during the previous week. The weekly status report—if done properly—could become one of the most important management tools available to junior, middle, and even senior managers. This is possible only if MIS managers consciously decide to create a good, workable format.

4.4.1 Guidelines for Weekly Reports

Even the most logical format is useless unless the procedures associated with weekly reporting are just as logical. Some excellent guidelines are:

1. In most organizations, no one weekly status report format will ever apply to all employees. Staff members have different roles and responsibilities at different times, and it is difficult to create one generalized status report that will handle everything from production support assignments to feasibility studies. If job responsibilities are significantly different, then management should provide significantly different weekly report formats.

2. Many MIS organizations have a built-in bias against having employees at the supervisory level and above fill out their own weekly reports. In those cases, staff members who have "made it" to a management position feel they no longer have to account for their time. This is a ridiculous assumption if management is truly concerned with the productivity of everyone in the department. MIS executives should insist that first- and second-level managers also complete weekly reports (their report formats should be designed specifically for management activities). A manager's time is just as valuable as the time spent by a programmer/analyst installing the new payroll system. In fact, one could argue that since managers are typically paid more than line employees, their time should be tracked more carefully!

3. A good form encourages two-way communication by allowing the employee to *initiate* informal dialogs or formal meetings with the manager. Every form should have a statement such as: Do you need to discuss anything with your manager? Even if the manager has a strong open-door policy, some employees may be reluctant to make the first move, and the paperwork can be their icebreaker.

4. Each weekly status report should be saved for use as an evaluation tool. When the inevitable question arises during the annual performance appraisal as to what exactly the employee has done, the manager should be ready with a stack of weekly reports in chronological order. One criteria for judging a form is its usefulness in employee evaluations. *If the manager cannot use the weekly report for performance evaluations, the form needs improvement.*

5. Warn employees that their weekly reports will be used in their performance appraisals. Although other factors will certainly enter into the final evaluation picture, the weekly report will be a major tool for grading achievements and progress toward previously assigned goals.

6. Every employee needs feedback concerning weekly reports, even if the manager simply says, "I can't read this line." If the manager even *appears* to ignore weekly reports, the employee may become careless and lose interest in tracking accomplishments. If the manager does not care about weekly reporting, neither will employees.

7. When staff members spend virtually all their time on a project, allow them to use the project control form as their weekly report. If another reporting method gives the manager a fair indication of the entire week's effort, the manager should never insist on duplicate reports. Procedures should be enforced, but only within reasonable limits. Common sense is a good yardstick for applying standards.

8. The form should indicate the goals for the next week, but goal setting is more complex than many people realize. MBO (management by objectives) is a powerful tool for directing and controlling human resources, but it can easily be misused. In extreme cases, employees and management alike can "play games" by manipulating plans in such a way as to show that they always meet their objectives. Their weekly goals may have been set so low that their success is virtually assured, whereas more ambitious staff members may have set personal goals beyond normal reach. The objective of dedicated employees should be to become fully productive, not to use the MBO approach to make themselves look good at the expense of the organization.

Goals should be required on every weekly report, but they must be closely monitored by the immediate manager. A true MBO program helps both staff members and managers improve their own performance, while rewarding superior effort. It never encourages or allows employees to use weekly reports to polish their public image.

4.4.2 Examples of Status Reports

Useful status reports come in several shapes and sizes. Figure 4.6 presents a weekly status report for a staff professional who has multiple assignments, such as a programmer/analyst doing production support tasks. Figure 4.7 is a status report for an individual who has consistent job responsibilities from week to week, such as data control technician or computer operator. Figure 4.8 is a status report for professionals engaged in high-level systems design, consulting, research, or management. The entries on

FORM DP-4

Wonderful Widgets, Inc.
Management Information Systems Division
WEEKLY STATUS REPORT

Name: _____ Section: ____ Date: ____

Period covered: Week ____ Month ____ Other ____

Primary assignment: _____

Do you want this report routed to anyone else? Whom?

1. List the tasks you have completed this week that have taken more than two hours of your time. Estimate the hours used. If you have notified the user or requester that the task has been completed, check the notified user column. Check the follow-up needed column if you need to spend additional time this week on that task.

TASK	START DATE	END DATE	HOURS USED	NOTIFIED USER	FOLLOW-UP NEEDED
____	____	____	____	____	_____
____	____	____	____	____	_____
____	____	____	____	____	_____
____	____	____	____	____	_____
____	____	____	____	____	_____

Figure 4.6 Weekly Status Report for a Multiple-Assignment Professional

2. List in general terms the tasks that have taken you less than two hours. Count the approximate number of times you performed each task this week. Indicate who or where the task came from, if that is appropriate. List any additional information in the comments column.

TASK	TIMES PERFORMED	SOURCE	COMMENTS
————	————	————	————
————	————	————	————
————	————	————	————
————	————	————	————
————	————	————	————
————	————	————	————
————	————	————	————

3. List the tasks in progress that will take more than two hours. Fill in the start date, estimated end date, a percentage complete estimate (in multiples of 10 percent), and a comment in the current status column that best describes your progress.

TASK	START DATE	EST. END DATE	% COMPLETE	CURRENT STATUS
———	———	———	————	———
———	———	———	————	———
———	———	———	————	———
———	———	———	————	———
———	———	———	————	———
———	———	———	————	———
———	———	———	————	———

Figure 4.6 (*Continued*)

4. Are you waiting for assistance or information from any other section, department, unit, or vendor that is holding up any of your assignments?

_____

_____

_____

5. List any roadblocks or potential roadblocks that were not listed in question 4. _____

_____

_____

6. What are your goals for this next reporting period? (Do not repeat information given in question 3.)

_____

_____

_____

_____

7. Prioritize your assignments. _____

_____

_____

8. Do you want to talk to your supervisor about this report?

Yes ____   No ____

9. Do you have any other important information about this past reporting period that has not been mentioned?

_____

_____

_____

Figure 4.6 Weekly Status Report for a Multiple-Assignment Professional (*Continued*)

FORM DP-5

Wonderful Widgets, Inc.
Management Information Systems Division
WEEKLY STATUS REPORT

Name: _____ Section: _____ Date: _____

Period covered: Week _____ Month _____ Other _____

Primary assignment: _____

1. List your general duties in the task column. Enter the approximate percentage of your time spent last week on that task. Use the A-B-C priority code, with A the highest and C the lowest. Use the comments space to provide additional information.

TASK	% OF TIME SPENT	PRTY	COMMENTS

2. Were any of your tasks not completed on time? If so, list the task and the reasons, if known.

_____

_____

_____

Figure 4.7 Weekly Report for Positions with Consistent Responsibilities

3. List any roadblocks or delays in completing your assignments.

_____

_____

_____

4. Do you have any additional information regarding the last reporting period, or any suggestions?

_____

_____

_____

_____

5. Do you want to talk to your supervisor about this report?

Yes ____   No ____

Figure 4.7 Weekly Report for Positions with Consistent Responsibilities (*Continued*)

FORM DP-6

Wonderful Widgets, Inc.
Management Information Systems Division
WEEKLY STATUS REPORT

Name: _____ Section: _____ Date: _____

Period covered: Week _____ Month _____ Other _____

Primary assignments: _____

_____

_____

1. In priority sequence (A-B-C), list your personal assignments. Estimate the percentage of your time spent on each task. Briefly summarize the status of each assignment.

ASSIGNMENT	% TIME	STATUS
_____	_____	_____
_____	_____	_____
_____	_____	_____
_____	_____	_____
_____	_____	_____
_____	_____	_____

2. What problems did you have last week that affected your work or your group's performance?

_____

_____

_____

_____

Figure 4.8 Weekly Report for a Manager or Senior Professional

3. Rate your own time management skills during the past reporting period.

Good ⎯⎯ Unsatisfactory ⎯⎯

Adequate ⎯⎯

Explain the reasons for an unsatisfactory rating.

_____

_____

4. What scheduled assignments did you complete last week? Do not include tasks assigned to subordinates or others, and do not include projects that are reported in other documents. List only personal accomplishments.

_____

_____

_____

5. List any personal time-critical assignments due during the next four weeks.

_____

_____

_____

6. If you manage people, are you caught up with your administrative requirements?

Yes ⎯⎯ No ⎯⎯

7. Do you have any additional information that should be discussed with your manager?

_____

_____

_____

Figure 4.8 Weekly Report for a Manager or Senior Professional (*Continued*)

each form are designed to match the typical activities of each generic group.

Notice that all three formats contain specific instructions as part of the form, which eliminates the need to have separate documents for instructions. This approach is useful in many other situations.

These three formats force employees to define their roles or "primary functions," their duties, and the relative priority of their assignments. Managers are forced to rate their own time management skills on a weekly basis. Again, the type of question asked on any status report should reflect the organization's attitude.

4.5 EXPERIENCE EVALUATION FORMS

When new employees start, one of the first and most important responsibilities of the senior staff is to accurately measure the experience and skill level of those new MIS staff members. Many experienced MIS managers feel that interviewing during the hiring process does not give supervisors a reliable picture of the potential employee, except in very general terms. Although progressive installations are now implementing careful prehiring screening techniques, many organizations still rely only on the classic interview procedure to categorize future employees. But without a standardized evaluation system, it may take weeks or even months for a supervisor to discover the true experience level or capabilities of the newly hired professional. This delay is now unacceptable to modern managers.

At the same time, management should periodically study the existing employees and determine both ongoing training needs and possible staff reassignments. When employees are evaluated in a standardized manner, the results can be compared from year to year or even from quarter to quarter. Such surveys also demonstrate individual growth or progress and can be used during performance reviews.

One excellent way to evaluate both new and current employees is through a written *skills survey* or *experience evaluation*. The title of the document is not important, but the purpose is vital: to take a "technical snapshot" of each employee so that the employee can be directed to the right training program or job assignment. The experience evaluation form can also be used as an interview screening device, if this is approved by the company's legal department. No interview material should violate (or even appear to violate) federal equal opportunity provisions, although documents that deal only with technical matters usually do not present problems in that area.

Figure 4.9 is a sample skills survey or experience evaluation form that can be used to screen new employees, analyze the current MIS staff, and look at potential reassignments. This particular example is oriented toward a large IBM mainframe installation with IMS; the surveys used in other types of organizations would reflect their own particular technical environments.

4.6 MONTHLY AND QUARTERLY REPORTS

Mention the subject of monthly or quarterly reports to most managers or senior-level staff members and they will frown, complain, groan, moan, or change the subject (or some combination thereof). Periodic status reports are looked on as the price one must pay for holding a supervisory or management-level position. Even a company president must prepare a monthly, quarterly, and yearly report for the board of directors or a similar group. Of course, senior-level company executives, such as company presidents, may have assistants to handle such dirty work, but the typical line manager has no such convenient escape.

However disliked the task, the job of writing a progress report is another opportunity to improve communication throughout the department. Managers who effectively communicate the status of their sections (which includes successes, failures, and everything in between) are looked on by their superiors as managers who successfully tell their story. Senior company managers frequently complain that data-processing executives live in their own independent

FORM DP-7
Wonderful Widgets, Inc.
Management Information Systems Division
PROFESSIONAL SKILLS SURVEY

Name: ———————————————— Date: —————

Section: ————————— Manager: ————————————

This questionnaire is not a test or performance evaluation. The purpose is to help us understand the training and experience needs of our professional staff. Please fill out sections I through IV and return the questionnaire to your manager within five working days.

    Thank you.

SECTION I:
GENERAL TECHNICAL EXPERIENCE

1. Check the operating systems you have used, and select the term that best describes your experience level.

SYSTEM	EXTENSIVE	MODERATE	MINIMAL
OS/VS1	___	___	___
VM	___	___	___
MVS	___	___	___
DOS/VS	___	___	___
DOS/VSE	___	___	___
DOS/SSX	___	___	___
Others:			
———	___	___	___
———	___	___	___
———	___	___	___

Figure 4.9 Experience Evaluation Form for the Systems and Programming Staff

2. What computers have you worked with?

MANUFACTURER/MODEL   **YEARS EXPERIENCE**

_____   _____

_____   _____

_____   _____

_____   _____

3. Describe any minicomputer or microcomputer experience. Include hardware, software, and languages.

_____

_____

_____

_____

_____

If you have never worked with a micro or mini, are you interested in a future opportunity in the mini or micro areas?

_____

_____

_____

4. Have you ever done any system software work, such as operating system or compiler "gens"?

_____

_____

_____

_____

Figure 4.9 Experience Evaluation Form for the Systems and Programming Staff (_Continued_)

5. Have you ever worked with IBM OS utility programs? If yes, describe the hardware/software configuration.

Check the utilities you have successfully used.

IEBPTPCH	___	IEBUPDTE	___
IEBCOPY	___	IEHLIST	___
IEBCOMPR	___	IEHMOVE	___
IEBDG	___	IEHPROGM	___
IEBGENER	___	IDCAMS	___
IEBISAM	___		

Which ones are you most confident with?

Have you had any formal training in utilities? If not, would you like a course or instruction in their use?

6. If you have worked with IBM OS JCL, check the areas, items, and concepts you are familiar with. Select the rating that best describes your experience level.

1: Very familiar
2: Can handle most situations without assistance
3: Have some experience, but occasionally need help
4: Very little experience, reading knowledge only

Figure 4.9 (Continued)

AREA	RATING	AREA	RATING
In-stream procs	_____	Reruns of production jobs	_____
Catalogued procs	_____	Restarted production jobs	_____
JCL overrides to procs	_____	Have written restart instructions	_____
Generation data groups	_____	Used symbolic parms to pass information to a proc	_____
Have written procs from scratch	_____	Modified production procs	_____
Worked with tape files	_____	Calculated disk space requirements	_____
Worked with disk files	_____	Determined backup/restore requirements	_____
Partitioned data sets (PDS)	_____		
ISAM	_____		
VSAM	_____		
Direct-access files	_____		

7. Check the software packages you have worked with.

LIBRARIAN	_____	TSO/SPF	_____
ROSCOE	_____	CLISTS	_____
RPFs	_____	CICS	_____
PANVALET	_____	IMS DL/I	_____
TSO	_____	IMS DB/DC	_____

Figure 4.9 Experience Evaluation Form for the Systems and Programming Staff (*Continued*)

Other data bases or TP monitors?

_____

_____

SAS _____ EASYTRIEVE _____

FOCUS _____

Other report writers or mainframe software packages?

_____

_____

_____

8. Have you worked with computer terminals? _____

Have you had any data entry experience? _____

Have you worked on systems requiring teleprocessing? If so, please describe.

_____

_____

9. Have you worked with any other hardware/software combinations not listed above, such as point-of-sale, direct order entry, or bank automated teller terminals?

_____

_____

10. Have you ever supported production jobs, such as payroll or general ledger?

_____

_____

Figure 4.9 (_Continued_)

If so, list the systems and describe the extent of your involvement.

_____

_____

_____

_____

11. Have you ever been "on call" in a production environment? If yes, describe your experience.

_____

_____

_____

12. Have you ever operated a computer? If so, list the computers and your experience.

_____

_____

_____

Are you interested in the hardware aspect of data processing? If so, please explain.

_____

_____

_____

13. Have you interfaced with an operations section? If so, describe your involvement.

_____

_____

Figure 4.9 Experience Evaluation Form for the Systems and Programming Staff (*Continued*)

14. Have you had design experience with:

Program or module design? _____

Integrated modules? _____

Complete systems? _____

Summarize your design experience.

_____

_____

_____

15. Over your entire career, how much direct user interface have you had?

None _____   Significant _____

Limited _____   Extensive _____

Do you like to work with users? _____

Describe your user contact—problem resolution, consulting, systems design, training, etc.

_____

_____

_____

_____

16. Have you worked with any purchased application system packages? If so, list them and your involvement.

_____

_____

_____

Figure 4.9 (Continued)

17. Have you debugged programs using core or memory dumps? If yes, rate your skill at solving problems through a core dump. Mention any automated packages or debugging tools you have used.

_____

_____

_____

_____

18. Have you written any system design proposals or done any feasibility studies? If so, describe your involvement.

_____

_____

_____

_____

_____

19. Please summarize your *previous* DP experience.

YEARS	COMPANY	COMPANY BUSINESS	DUTIES
___	_____	_____	_____
___	_____	_____	_____
___	_____	_____	_____
___	_____	_____	_____
___	_____	_____	_____
___	_____	_____	_____

Figure 4.9 Experience Evaluation Form for the Systems and Programming Staff (*Continued*)

SECTION II:
LANGUAGES AND DATA BASE

If you are now using PL/I or have used PL/I in the past, please answer all the questions in this group:

1. How many years of experience do you have with PL/I? _____

2. What version(s) have you used? _____

_____

_____

3. Check the terms you can define and discuss in detail:

Based variables	_____	DSA	_____
Controlled storage	_____	TCA	_____
Index area	_____	Regional (1)	_____
Fixed overflow	_____	Recursive	_____
Oncode 8097	_____	Aligned	_____
Pointer	_____	External variable	_____
Static	_____	Order/reorder	_____
Dynamic allocation	_____		

Are you familiar with these concepts?

Based I/O	_____	Substr	_____
Record I/O	_____	PLIRETC	_____
"By name" option	_____	PL/I internal sorts	_____
Label variables	_____	Allocate	_____
Two-dimension tables	_____		

Figure 4.9 (Continued)

4. How do you rate your general knowledge of PL/I? (Check one of the following five statements.)

Can handle almost all requirements of PL/I ‎ _____

Can handle most PL/I requirements ‎ _____

Good knowledge of PL/I, but need help ‎ _____

Can read PL/I and understand logic ‎ _____

Minimal knowledge of PL/I ‎ _____

5. How good is your ability to read and debug PL/I core dumps?

_____

What do you think of PL/I programming in general?

_____

_____

_____

6. What do you need in terms of PL/I training? Please be as specific as possible.

_____

_____

_____

_____

If you are now using ASSEMBLER or have used it in the past, please answer all the questions in this group:

1. How many years ASSEMBLER experience do you have? _____

Figure 4.9 Experience Evaluation Form for the Systems and Programming Staff (*Continued*)

2. On what operating system(s)?

_____

3. Which instructions can you use?

MVC _____   IM _____   BAL _____

BALR _____   CVD _____   CVB _____

SRDL _____   BCT _____   EDMK _____

MVI _____   LR _____   STH _____

LM _____   EX _____   MP _____

4. In a core dump, can you pick out zoned decimal, packed, and binary numbers?

_____

5. With which of the following are you familiar?

Packed decimal arithmetic _____

Fixed-point arithmetic _____

Boolean logic and its use _____

Variable records _____

PDSs _____

Direct-access files _____

QSAM _____

BSAM _____

QISAM _____

QTAM _____

EXCP coding _____

TCAM _____

Figure 4.9 (_Continued_)

Graphics-access method _____

Changing a JFCB _____

Writing your own macros _____

Reentrant coding _____

6. What are your strongest areas of ASSEMBLER programming?

_____

_____

_____

7. In what areas do you need more training or experience?

_____

_____

_____

If you currently use COBOL or have used it in the past, please answer all the questions in this group:

1. How many years of COBOL experience do you have?

_____

2. What version(s) of COBOL have you used? Under what CPUs and what operating systems?

_____

_____

_____

_____

Figure 4.9 Experience Evaluation Form for the Systems and Programming Staff (*Continued*)

3. Check the terms you can define and discuss in detail.

Comp	___	Move	___
Tallying	___	Set (index)	___
Renames	___	Comp-2	___
Search	___	Exit	___
Group indicate	___	Perform	___
Comp-3	___	Compute	___
Occurs	___		

4. Are you familiar with these topics?

Report writer   ___

ISAM files   ___

Direct-access files ___

Calling ASSEMBLER modules from COBOL   ___

5. How would you rate your COBOL skills? Are they adequate to perform your current job functions?

_____

_____

_____

_____

6. What would you like to see in terms of COBOL training?

_____

_____

_____

Figure 4.9 (Continued)

7. Can you debug COBOL modules from a core dump?

_____

If you have used IMS, please answer these questions:

1. Check the terms you can discuss in detail.

Root segment	_____	Command code	_____
PCB	_____	PSB	_____
SENSEG	_____	PSBGEN	_____
GU	_____	GNP	_____
DLET	_____	ISRT	_____
Unqualified SSA	_____	Qualified SSA	_____
Multiple PCBs	_____		

2. List the four types of IMS access methods.

_____

_____

_____

_____

_____

_____

3. What would you like in terms of additional IMS training?

_____

_____

_____

_____

Figure 4.9 Experience Evaluation Form for the Systems and Programming Staff (*Continued*)

SECTION III:
APPLICATION SYSTEMS EXPERIENCE

Use the following scale to rate yourself on a combination of experience and knowledge of business application systems. Remember that different companies have different names for the same business functions. Your rating should include both current experience and previous employment.

0: None
1: Very little
2: Some experience but limited knowledge
3: Practical working experience
4: Good experience and knowledge
5: Excellent experience

A.	Payroll	0	1	2	3	4	5
B.	General ledger	0	1	2	3	4	5
C.	Accounts payable	0	1	2	3	4	5
D.	Accounts receivable	0	1	2	3	4	5
E.	Profit and loss	0	1	2	3	4	5
F.	Inventory control	0	1	2	3	4	5
G.	Open orders	0	1	2	3	4	5
H.	Sales reporting	0	1	2	3	4	5
I.	Forecasting	0	1	2	3	4	5
J.	Order processing	0	1	2	3	4	5
K.	Warehouse control	0	1	2	3	4	5
L.	Warehouse scheduling	0	1	2	3	4	5
M.	Billing/invoicing	0	1	2	3	4	5
N.	Purchase orders	0	1	2	3	4	5
O.	Bill of materials	0	1	2	3	4	5
P.	MRP	0	1	2	3	4	5
Q.	Shop floor control	0	1	2	3	4	5
R.	Automatic data collection	0	1	2	3	4	5
S.	Automated storage/retrieval systems	0	1	2	3	4	5

Figure 4.9 (Continued)

Can you define these terms?

A. Purchase orders   _____

B. Open order   _____

C. Billing invoice   _____

D. Warehouse slot   _____

E. Back order   _____

F. Journal entry   _____

G. Chart of accounts   _____

H. General ledger account _____

I. Payroll check register   _____

J. Offsetting entry   _____

K. Picking document   _____

L. Wholesale distributor   _____

In general, how do you rate your current knowledge of the application systems you are working with? Would you like any specific training or education?

_____

_____

_____

_____

_____

_____

_____

_____

Figure 4.9 Experience Evaluation Form for the Systems and Programming Staff (*Continued*)

SECTION IV:
TRAINING NEEDS

Please list any ideas, comments, or suggestions for a training and internal education program, especially as it relates to your own situation.

_____

_____

_____

_____

_____

Thank you. Please return this form to your manager.

SECTION V:
MANAGER'S COMMENTS

(To be filled out by the employee's supervisor or manager.)

Please review the ratings and information in the first four sections. Can you add any more detail or suggestions for this individual?

_____

_____

_____

_____

_____

_____

_____

Figure 4.9 (_Continued_)

worlds, and one reason for that negative feeling is that MIS managers simply do not communicate well. In some cases, they do not communicate at all! Logically designed monthly and quarterly reports will go a long way toward reducing that serious communications gap.

The underlying tone of a monthly report is very important. The author must honestly state the situation without painting either too bleak or too optimistic a picture. The most effective monthly reports avoid emotion and present the facts objectively, letting readers draw their own conclusions. Some managers try to use the monthly or quarterly report as a tool to intimidate or blame others in the organization. This approach rarely works; in many situations it will earn a nasty reputation for the writer and outright sympathy for the victim. If the author has accusatory or similar statements, they should be saved for private documents. As a general rule, the writer should only make statements in a report that could be comfortably made directly to another person. If a statement (or accusation) fails this test, it should be removed from the monthly report.

4.6.1 Proper Handling of the Monthly Reports

Section and departmental reports should be public documents if at all possible. With the recent trend toward "participatory management" (and the desire to improve the flow of communication between management and employees), the author should distribute reports to at least the next level down in the corporate hierarchy. Second- or third-level managers can also give each member of their groups an individual copy of their own reports. Whereas management experts differ in their opinions on the amount and type of information that should be spread throughout the organization, most executives believe that a monthly or quarterly status report should be given to the manager's immediate subordinates.

Formal monthly reports must have correct grammar and syntax and a logical sentence structure. When managers do not have the basic writing skills to create a readable document, they should either develop those skills before the next month-end report or ask a qualified person to edit their work. No matter how productive and impressive the accomplishments, a poorly written progress report will always leave some feelings of frustration and disappointment.

A monthly or quarterly report longer than two pages needs a summary paragraph as the first entry. The size of the pages or the amount of information packed into each page makes little difference. Thanks to human nature, many people prefer to read summaries rather than detail, and a length of two pages seems to be the cross-over point between the two. Monthly reports are usually given to other managers or even employees outside of the MIS department who may not have the desire or time to read a four-page monthly report. Frank Flowchart may write his monthly report for MIS Director Shelly Super, but he may also give copies to Tina Template and Lana Ledger. Both Tina and Lana will learn more about Frank's work from a short summary that they actually read than from a four-page report they throw in the wastebasket. *People generally do read summaries.*

4.6.2 Sample Monthly Report

The following is a general-purpose format that can handle a wide variety of MIS activities, including production support, project development, operations, and a combination of those functions. Again, senior management must insist that all departments and sections follow a standard format so that reports from one level can be combined with other reports to feed the next-higher reporting level. Programming managers should be able to easily combine and condense the reports from their unit managers into their own departmental monthly reports. MIS directors should also be able to combine and condense the various department reports into their own final divisional monthly reports. This practice works successfully only if there are standardized report formats. A typical format would be:

1. Summary
2. Major accomplishments
3. Major project status
4. Activity summary
5. Major goals for the next period
6. Progress toward quarterly or yearly goals
7. Problems
8. Conclusions

Summary. Develop if needed.

Major accomplishments. A major accomplishment is one that required significant effort or had a definite impact on the department, a customer, or the product. In some installations, the term "major accomplishment" varies so much from manager to manager that one report may list ten pages of "major accomplishments" while another mentions only three items. At face value, the department with ten pages of major accomplishments appears to be doing a better job than a department with only three major tasks. This, of course, may be nonsense. Unless senior management carefully defines (and enforces) the category of major accomplishments," the individual monthly reports may be worthless for comparison purposes.

Major project status. Most units in MIS have at least one important project that has taken or will take more than one calendar month. Such projects need a separate discussion in the monthly report that does not repeat information in the major accomplishments section, but rather summarizes the general status. The writer should also state whether the project is on, ahead of, or behind schedule and the reasons for any deviation from the plan.

Activity summary. This section analyzes the time spent by the group or unit in terms of planned and unplanned activities. Such events as training, vacations, and education are known events that can be planned for with appropriate scheduling. Unplanned events such as an illness or a sudden request for a programmer's time to help with a critical data base abend cannot be anticipated, but they are just as important in explaining how employees spent their time.

The activity summary is often the hardest section to write, but it can be the most enlightening. After all, company management continually asks the question: How do all those people spend their time? The activity summary should answer that question in no uncertain terms.

Major goals for the next period. A "goal" section should contain the manager's best guess as to the objectives that can reasonably be expected by the end of the next reporting period. If the goals are not reasonable but must be scheduled anyway, the employee should carefully mention that the goals are *time-critical*. This notifies all readers of the sensitive commitment and leaves no room for ignorance.

Only important goals that meet the requirements of "major accomplishments" should be included. Exceptions may be those relatively small but critical objectives that affect other departments or that entail legal obligations.

Progress toward quarterly or yearly goals. This section will analyze the progress made toward meeting formal goals. If no progress has been made, or if the department is falling behind in meeting those objectives, the reasons can be discussed in this section.

The purpose is to make sure that all units in the division are aware of their long-term goals and are periodically evaluating their progress toward those objectives.

Problems. This section contains a list of the problems or roadblocks that have surfaced in four areas:

Planned intermittent

Planned recurring

Unplanned intermittent

Unplanned recurring

"Planned" implies that the manager knew in advance of the situation. "Intermittent" suggests a problem that occurs sporadically or on a one-time basis. "Recurring" describes a problem that has occurred more than once during the reporting period.

This four-way separation of problems forces the writer to categorize those roadblocks in terms that will help to effectively plan for the future. After listing the problems, the author can propose solutions either in the monthly report or in another document.

Conclusions. The last section contains the personal opinion of the manager or author and should answer the general question: How is the department doing in relation to its objectives? Whereas the other sections concentrate on facts and measurable events, the conclusion section is the appropriate place for value judgments. Ideally, the previous factual statements will support these conclusions.

Since a monthly or quarterly report should be a public document, the author should avoid appearing either too pessimistic or overly optimistic. Rather, the attitude presented should be one of positive professionalism.

4.7 MEMOS

If written communication is truly the lifeblood of modern business, the popular memo is either the vital nourishment that keeps the body going or the garbage that clogs up the arteries. Some companies have so many memos floating from person to person that their employees spend more time writing memos than performing their job functions. Other organizations discourage memos and rely on verbal communication. Such negative attitudes toward memos are usually the result of tradition or experience rather than any formal management directive. Memos are not intrinsically good or bad. But if used properly, they can be more than just another necessary evil.

It is easy to overuse memos and ignore the telephone or face-to-face communication. Personal discussions can solve many problems, obtain information, and present ideas in a relatively efficient manner. Verbal communication is best used for taking preliminary steps toward an agreement that will eventually be documented. Memos, however, are another method of explaining, presenting, and settling the important issues in the MIS division.

4.7.1 Memos as a Business Tool

Many people who deal with memos never realize that memos themselves can cause extra work. The reader may not be sure what to do with a particular memo. Is it for information only, or does it require a reply? When should the response be made? Is the memo time critical? Must the entire memo be read, even if it contains five pages of boring detail the reader barely understands? How does it affect the reader and the reader's work? Employees dealing with a flood of paperwork and reports can waste incalculable hours pondering those questions, even if they are never verbalized. When busy people receive another memo, their first reaction may be: What do I do with it? Such questions not only waste time, they often lead to the wrong course of action. *Productivity is enhanced when the recipient knows immediately what to do with a piece of paper.*

The solution is twofold. First, the author of the memo must answer the question for every recipient: What do I do with it? If the author does not know what action is expected, then why send the piece of paper or electronic massage? Second, the format of the memo must allow the author to pass along the information in a simple and nonthreatening manner. The recipient may not agree with the "disposition" suggestions of the author, but at least the author should establish a starting point.

Figure 4.10 presents a memo heading format that allows the writer to express action recommendations for each individual.

Using the *requested disposition* feature is complicated when writing to a nonsubordinate. The author cannot simply order the respondent to reply by a certain date; one does not *tell* a person higher in the pecking order or in another

FORM DP-8

Wonderful Widgets, Inc.
Management Information Systems
INTERNAL MEMO

To: _____ From: _____ Date: _____

Subject: _____

Filing subject, if different: _____

DISTRIBUTION LIST:

NAME	DEPT	Requested disposition		
		REPLY BY	ACTION BY	FYI
_____	_____	_____	_____	__
_____	_____	_____	_____	__
_____	_____	_____	_____	__
_____	_____	_____	_____	__
_____	_____	_____	_____	__
_____	_____	_____	_____	__

MESSAGE:

_____

_____

_____

_____

_____

_____

_____

_____

Figure 4.10 Standard Internal Memo

department what to do. A way to avoid the problem is to leave the date blank in the heading but suggest a date in the body of the text. If the date is phrased in the form of a question, the recipient probably will not be insulted. For example, one might say, "If possible, can you respond by September 14?" When writing to colleagues, a systems analyst would specify a requested disposition date, but when writing to the MIS Director, the analyst would suggest a date in the memo. Tact is always wise, especially when writing to one's own manager.

Memos should contain a *filing subject* heading, because the subject listed may not indicate the overall category under which it should be filed. Using standardized filing subjects allows employees to set up filing systems that match those of the rest of the company. If all memos that pertain to the Worm Farm Management System project are so labeled, one staff member will not file those memos in a file called "Worms" while another saves the documents in a file labeled "Muddy Flats, Iowa, Project." The increase in efficiency is amazing!

The body of a memo should use an outline form, because the sequential nature of an outline communicates more efficiently than straight text. A memo should rarely be written in narrative prose; rather, it should be similar to a user manual, with frequent headings, clearly delineated sections, and no unnecessary words and phrases. A good memo may even seem choppy during the first reading, but that feeling of conciseness does not interfere with communication. Memos should never use excess words! They should be brief, concise, and relevant.

Any memo more than two pages long (no matter how much longer) requires a summary. Busy managers and professionals will often choose between reading a summary and tossing the memo in their "in" baskets. Summaries are read more often than complete memos. Writing the summary also helps the authors condense their thoughts and focus on the true purpose of their documents.

4.7.2 A Sample Memo

The following example communicates effectively:

FORM DP-8

Wonderful Widgets, Inc.
Management Information Systems
INTERNAL MEMO

To: C. Crawly   From: T. Template   Date: 09/05/85

Subject: Billing Amounts

Filing subject, if different: Worm Farm Management System

DISTRIBUTION LIST:

| | | Requested disposition | | |
NAME	DEPT	REPLY BY	ACTION BY	FYI
C. Crawly	Dirt Ent.	9/24	9/24	
S. Slimy	Dirt Ent.			x
L. Ledger	Acct			x
S. Super	MIS			x

MESSAGE:

As you know, Carl, we are completing the system design for the Worm Farm Management System (WOFMS). One final requirement is to verify the size estimates you and Sara gave us last year. Once I have the final estimates, I will work with Lana and calculate the billing charges. Basically, Wonderful Widgets charges internal users according to the total of transaction charges, the file storage charge, and the additional hardware needed. This amount is then charged as a direct operating expense in the general ledger.

Please answer the following questions:

Transaction Volumes
1. How many adult worms are born during a peak month?
2. How many times a month do you need to change the characteristics of a given adult worm, such as color or weight?
3. How many married adult worms die as a result of natural causes every month? (Is their higher death rate the result of stress-related illnesses caused by pressures to support their families?)
4. How often do your employees accidentally squish the little creatures? Remember, we agreed that an accidental squishing would require separate updates to the Worm Master data base and the Homicide data base.

File Storage
1. How many worms are in storage during slow, normal, and peak months?
2. In your Beautiful Worm data base, how many shades of brown will you track?

I realize this is partially a duplicate of information you supplied last year, but I need current values before we can compute our internal charge-out rates.

If you have any questions, please contact me at 555-7453, extension W-O-R-M. Thanks again for your help.

The preceding memo was a simple request for data from a user. Other memos can convey information, argue a case, propose a solution, discuss a problem, or merely stimulate thinking. Whatever the purpose, a good memo should always avoid unnecessary words or phrases.

One important note on the subject of memos: A good rule is to consider a telephone call or personal visit before writing a memo. Will either of those two methods accomplish the same result?

4.8 UNPLEASANT NEWS

Most professionals face situations in which they must inform their manager or another executive of some unpleasant news. Such information may concern a cost overrun, a system design that overlooked a key point, a rejected idea, or an opinion that obviously goes against the manager's thinking. Although some human relations experts suggest that bad news is best given in person, there are many occasions when those embarrassing cost overruns must be discussed in writing.

The first advice for any writer in that situation is to proceed cautiously. Never write a memo or report when angry, upset, or frustrated. Most organizations do not need memos that sound angry, upset, or frustrated, because such documents trigger unproductive emotional responses. The only thing worse than an angry employee is an angry employee facing an equally angry manager. Both may be losers in the end.

The second bit of advice is to gently prepare the reader before the paperwork arrives. The author should warn the recipient that a memo or report with unpleasant news will be arriving and should request a meeting to discuss the problem. Suddenly handing a senior vice president a memo stating that the new order entry system is $200,000 over budget and may be six months late will certainly trigger a negative emotional reaction. A carefully planned phone call to warn the reader will usually defuse a potentially explosive situation.

The third suggestion is to always write in a style that does not blame or condemn. If the author must contradict the manager's statements, the memo can mention both sides of the issue. People respond better when the written word does not threaten or attack them personally. Above all, never insert comments that can be interpreted as personal criticism. In the world of internal company communications, each matter should be judged on its own merits.

4.9 SUMMARY OF KEY POINTS

☐ Internal forms and documents are a direct reflection of management policy—if the formats are ineffective, management itself may be equally ineffective. If the forms are well designed (under management supervision), they will help implement management policy.

☐ The user service request form needs a simple identification scheme that conveys more than the sequence in which it was received.

☐ A service request form should come with detailed, explicit instructions. Some users will not "automatically" understand.

☐ Project control status reports have two purposes: (1) to help staff members accurately pinpoint their status and (2) to communicate that information to management.

☐ The project management form should be easy to fill out, positive in nature, and professionally prepared.

☐ A standardized task control method is essential for employees who have multiple assignments. Don't allow those staff members to try to keep everything in their heads.

☐ Professionals with differing responsibilities need different weekly report forms. Requiring all employees to use the same weekly report form is a mistake.

☐ The manager should provide *weekly* feedback on the employee's *weekly* report. Never let a report go unanswered.

☐ Interviews alone do not give employers an accurate picture of a potential employee's technical skills. An experience evaluation form will quickly fill in the details. Those forms should also be used in a continuing program of employee measurement.

☐ The author of a memo should indicate in the heading exactly what action each recipient is expected to take, along with a target date for that action.

☐ Before giving unpleasant news in a memo, the author should prepare the recipient verbally. One should never compose a memo while in an angry or emotional state. Technical and business documents should be built on facts rather than emotion.

chapter **5**

User Manuals:
Preparation

User manuals come in several forms: the traditional paper document, online HELP functions, and computer-assisted instruction. Yet they all require the same degree of careful preparation and planning. This chapter shows the technical writer how to gather knowledge about a subject, understand the limitations and capabilities of the audience, and obtain willing cooperation from the users. The chapter reviews the serious questions: Who controls user manuals, and should manuals be standardized? Technical writers, systems analysts, users, and MIS managers will find the correct procedures for starting a user manual documentation project.

Requirements documents and business plans are more

visible, but the often underated user manual can make the difference between the ultimate success and failure of a computerized system. Even the best application, product, or device is worthless unless the users can operate the system effectively. User manuals may be an afterthought. Too many MIS directors and managers classify a project as "complete" even if the user manual phase is not finished or the final document itself is unacceptable to the end consumers. But MIS as a profession is painfully learning that true service to the users includes providing them with high-quality operating instructions and training.

Many user complaints about an application come from misunderstandings or confusion about the capabilities and restrictions of the product. The specific application may actually work perfectly! In fact, much of the expensive, unnecessary maintenance effort in some installations is caused by a lack of correct, understandable, and practical user documentation. Maintenance project leaders report example after example of wasted programmer effort because the user did not "understand" the system. The fault may not lie with the users—if MIS has not delivered good documentation, the users have nothing to work with. From a long-range management viewpoint, *MIS can often justify projects for developing user manuals on the basis of reduced maintenance costs.*

Another common problem with user manuals is their lack of *currency.* A manual that was accurate five years ago may lead users merrily down the wrong path if the manual has not been kept up to date. Other manuals may be current, but the technical writer or other author may not have understood the system well enough to tell others how to properly use it. Simply having a manual is not enough. *Incorrect user instructions are often worse than no instructions at all.*

5.1   TYPES OF USER MANUALS

User manuals are not limited to the traditional hard-copy format. In recent years the new online style of user documentation has proven quite successful. The classic example of this approach is the HELP facility of IBM's widely used TSO application, development, and support product for MVS and other IBM operating systems. Using HELP, the computer user (who may not be technically oriented) progresses through various levels of instructions that relate to TSO features. That is, if assistance is needed while using a specific option, the user presses a key and the computer provides online documentation. In effect, the user manual has been put online and gives "automatic direct access" to the user. But HELP and similar online facilities are still a form of user manual and have the same problems as their cousins stored in traditional paper notebooks.

Computer-aided instruction (CAI) is now being implemented and will soon trigger a revolution in both training and documentation. When combined with direct frame access videodisk, CAI not only can teach a subject, it can provide an efficient way to deliver needed information to a user. In fact, one can foresee the day when "online manuals" and CAI/videodisk will replace most hard-copy manuals—paper, after all, is only a communications medium, and if technical writers discover a better approach, they should follow their ideas. Paper replaced the stone tablet and it may be time for something else to replace paper!

Manuals (both hard-copy and online) range in size from large volumes explaining a general ledger system to ten-line descriptions on how to hook up a CRT. The difference is quantitative rather than qualitative. While the author of the three-volume general ledger documentation faces additional problems related to dealing with large manuals, the technical writer scribbling the ten-line "quicky" instructions has the same goal: *User instructions must give the user the necessary information—no more and no less.* Deciding what the user truly needs may be complicated, but the principles and considerations behind effective user communication remain the same. One project may take six months while another takes six minutes, but both will have the same objectives.

5.2 HOW TO LEARN THE SUBJECT

Before technical writing became a separate profession, programmers were often drafted to write user documentation. In other cases, reluctant users volunteered to write their own manuals, and the results were predictable. The author knew the application (and perhaps even wrote it!) but did a poor job communicating this knowledge. In the 1980s the situation is reversed: technical writers and systems analysts have the writing skills, but they often lack a detailed understanding of their topics. Most professional writers have neither the technical ability nor the time to read program code and decipher a system from start to finish. Even programmers assigned to an application seldom accomplish that feat. Then how can a writer learn a system, application, or new computer in a reasonably efficient manner?

The first step is to contact a wide variety of acknowledged "experts" in the particular application. Most MIS departments have programmers, analysts, managers, data entry clerks, computer operators, or secretaries who have worked with the system and have some understanding of the product. They may know only the portions of the application that relate to their particular job functions, but they can be valuable allies. If the MIS organization functions in a closed manner and does not encourage "knowledge sharing," the technical writer must work through official channels to obtain commitments from other managers. It is an absolute requirement for any technical author to utilize internal MIS resources *before* going outside the department.

From a logical standpoint, the more information an author possesses before going to the users, the better that author can relate to those users and understand their problems. *Nothing infuriates (and disappoints) a busy user more than an MIS professional who has obviously not done the necessary homework.* MIS staffers—whether they are programmers, analysts, technical writers, managers, or MIS directors—make both themselves and the department look unprofessional if they have not gathered the basic information before meeting the user. Since technical authors need user respect when working on such projects, they must avoid seeming incompetent.

The second step is to play "detective" and locate all available written documentation on the system within MIS. Despite loud protests from cynical programmers and analysts, most shops *do* have *some* written documentation on virtually every production system. It may be written on five-year-old paper yellowed with age or typed by a sleepy programmer at three in the morning. It may be scribbled on tab cards, stuck on a bulletin board, or forgotten in an old online library. But written information usually does exist, and those notes, memos, and assorted documents are valuable reference tools. The information may be out-of-date or even totally incorrect, but the terminology, descriptions, and attitudes will prepare the technical writer for discussions with internal MIS staff members and users. Discovering hard-to-find and unorganized documentation is often a challenge, but the results are worth the effort.

As a supplement to written material, the best tool to gather information for a technical writer is a tape recorder. If approached cautiously (and if the practice is allowed by company policy), many MIS employees will agree to a recording session if their statements are to be used only for information purposes. *The technical writer must never violate this trust.* A programmer, for example, may have a deep understanding of the system flow but may hesitate to document this knowledge. With a microphone the technical writer can often get large amounts of information from such "experts" on tape while concentrating on asking the questions rather than transcribing the answers.

A third step is to schedule formal discussions with internal MIS experts and to plan the questions before the meetings. This is an excellent opportunity to verify facts listed on those assorted notes, memos, and documents. But the primary purpose of these short discussions is to prepare the writer to meet the users. The programmer, analyst, or manager can answer such questions as:

1. What is the purpose of the system?
2. How long have you been involved with it?
3. What is your function in relation to this system?
4. Can you summarize the processing?
5. Can you summarize the processing as the users see it?
6. Do you have any written information about this system?
7. Do you know anyone else who has written documentation?
8. What are the major strengths of the system?
9. What are the major weaknesses?
10. Do the users like this application? If not, which ones do not?
11. Does MIS have any special problems with the system?
12. Do the users need information about other applications in order to use this system?
13. What changes have taken place during the past few years?
14. Do the users have any ongoing requests or serious complaints related to this system or its operation?

Obviously, many of the preceding questions do not directly affect the creation of a user manual. Yet the answers are just as critical as a list of transaction codes or error messages, because virtually every user documentation project requires the author to develop a positive relationship with the user community. In most cases, *unless authors understand the "total" situation, they will not receive full cooperation, and their projects will suffer.* The author must *know* that MIS has been promising the accounting department a new general ledger system for the past five years *before* walking into Accounting and asking for help documenting the current general ledger system.

Meetings with internal experts should generally be short

(an hour or less) to avoid monopolizing technical personnel. Associates are usually willing to donate a quick hour or so to help a colleague, but a requested three-hour session may be put off until the next cold day in August. Even if the expert did agree to a three-hour intensive session, the technical writer may be unfamiliar with the terminology and concepts and may develop "information overload" very quickly. Short, informal discussions are most productive for everyone.

5.3 UNDERSTAND THE AUDIENCE

"Know your audience" may sound like a trite, simplified command similar to "know yourself," but preparing to write a user manual requires a detailed analysis of the potential readers. The analysis is not difficult if the author follows a standardized approach:

Have the users previously worked with the application, computer, or system? If they have no direct or recent experience, the author will be writing for naive users and must anticipate very basic questions. Sophisticated users do not generally need such detailed assistance.

Will all the users have the same level of experience? If the manual is for new users as well as experts, the author should consider a two-level approach whereby the manual has separate sections for the two types of users. Each section (which may be only a paragraph) can have a different vocabulary, sentence structure, and degree of detail. Another solution is to write *two* user manuals. Whatever the approach, one cannot write for new users in the same way one writes for sophisticated users.

How much judgment is required in using the system? Application systems differ significantly in the degree and nature of the judgment exercised by the users. For example, a technical writer would work with a different mindset when creating a manual for a decision support system (DSS) used by a CPA or MBA than would be used when developing a manual for warehouse forklift operators. Both groups make decisions when working with various screens on their computer terminals, but the CPAs and MBAs are probably more familiar with complex logic interactions. The author of the forklift operator manual would define in detail the possible alternatives when the operator discovers an out-of-stock condition, whereas the writer of a DSS manual would assume that the readers will develop their own possibilities. This is an extreme example, but the principle is valid: The technical writer must estimate the decision-making ability of the audience, because it will partially determine both the information provided and the literary style.

In most cases, the degree of decision making tends to increase as computer applications move away from the so-called bread-and-butter systems, such as payroll and general ledger, to the most sophisticated packages, such as merchandise analysis and decision support systems. In addition, even the technical aspects are changing. Programmers now use complex data-base calls that require careful planning before they begin coding. The way one codes an IMS program, for example, can dramatically affect the operating characteristics of a major update or inquiry module.

As the applications themselves become more complicated, technical writers find themselves relying more on the programming staff for answers. A good example is a writer developing a manual on data-base design—the author may need to depend totally on the experts for the necessary information.

Are the people reading the manual fully dedicated to the system? An order entry clerk whose main job is to enter customer orders must be approached differently than a nurse in a medical office who operates a microcomputer on an occasional basis. The amount of dedication partially determines the amount of detail and the degree of repetition. The less time a user consistently spends with the task in question, the more detailed the instructions should be.

The situation is worse when the user must juggle several tasks at the same time, and the technical writer must *try to view the manual from the user's position.* The pediatric nurse answering a phone with one hand and taking the temperature of a screaming three-year-old with the other does not have time to "go back to section III-A when the invalid patient number message appears." What does the nurse actually need at that point in time? Can the documentation provide enough detail in a condensed manner so that the nurse can handle the phone conversation, quiet the screaming three-year-old, and correct the CRT error simultaneously?

In such hectic environments, the manual should have virtually stand-alone sections that provide all the required information in one place. The author must repeat essential information when necessary. *Although the concept of stand-alone sections involves repetition of information and introduces the problem of maintainability, the practice is more than justified; the technical writer pays the price rather than the user.* But when writing for dedicated users who will be thoroughly familiar with both the application and documentation, the author can legitimately send the reader back to other sections for additional information. Repetition can then be avoided.

Can the users get help easily, and what form will that help take? Consider a technical writer documenting a microcomputer-based inventory control system. The package will be sold with the hardware as a turnkey system, and the users may be 3000 miles away. The software company has a "hotline" but wants to reserve it for serious problems. Should the manual be as complete as is humanly possible? Of course!

Other writing assignments involve situations in which the user facing the computer monster does have access to people who can answer questions. A bank teller having trouble with an online cash transaction certainly has knowledgeable supervisors who can provide additional information or advice. Although the author should still provide a relatively complete set of teller-oriented information, it is safe to assume that the user will never be totally alone.

Are the users generally motivated? If the typical users of a particular system are generally unmotivated, the technical writer can perform a service for the company by adding both spirit and humor to the documentation. Who says the *Guide to AJAX SOFTWARE General Ledger and Window Washing System* must be totally boring? Humor—as long as it does not interfere with communication of essential facts and ideas—is perfectly acceptable.

Why can't this manual have a lighthearted story about Joyce Journal, who can never balance payroll entries, or about Gary Gremlin, who occasionally causes the funny little red light to appear on the disk drive control unit? To make Gary Gremlin go away, the user can simply hit the reset button and reboot the system. The average nontechnical user would rather read about a red light called Gary Gremlin than about a "channel control interface warning" light (or CCIW). Obviously, the manual must also have the correct name for reference purposes. Computers, like technical documentation, are not required by a law of nature to be dull. Each one of us has a little child within, and a touch of humor in a user manual can actually help frustrated users view their jobs with a more positive attitude.

5.4 GETTING COOPERATION AT THE START

The success of many technical writing assignments ultimately depends on the cooperation of the users. As technical writers follow their own professional paths and move away from the traditional programming and systems background, they will need even more help.

Logically, obtaining cooperation from users should be extremely easy. Many writing assignments deal with revising and updating existing user manuals, and the readers are personally interested in having better documentation. They never hesitate to point out problems and suggest improvements. In many cases they will demand rather than suggest!

But occasionally the technical writer faces an uncooperative or negative user who hinders rather than helps the project. The underlying cause may be a long-running dissatisfaction with the current user manual or even with MIS in general. Frustrated users who are negative toward MIS will transfer their hostilities without hesitation to the innocent technical writer standing in the doorway. Such situations are complex, politically dangerous, and personally frustrating for the writer. In many cases, the author must simply do the best job possible under very difficult circumstances. As a last resort, a request can be made for management pressure on the reluctant individuals.

Getting off to a good start with users requires a logical plan of action that recognizes their responsibilities as part of an interdepartment team:

Notify the appropriate individuals and their managers of the project. The technical writer should never rush over to the users, announce the start of a project to upgrade their system's user manual, and demand instant suggestions. The notification process is somewhat involved, because writers must not only give the users time to think about revisions to their manual, they must make sure that the *correct* users are brought into the picture. The boss, however important, may not be the best user to work with in documenting a particular application.

Depending on their particular management philosophy, *some managers consider themselves experts* in all aspects of their departments' operation *and will ignore staff people* who may be the *users* most qualified to help with a documentation project. The implications are serious! A technical writer forced to work with a manager or supervisor who is at best a casual user will often miss useful information. The most effective response is to gently encourage the manager to allow the technical writer open access to those employees who can truly provide assistance. If the user-manager insists on dealing with the technical writer personally even though it is obvious that the manager is not qualified, the writer should discuss the problem with MIS management. Postponing or even canceling the project is then an unfortunate but logical alternative.

Schedule a meeting to present the purpose, nature, and scope of the documentation project. The writer needs a carefully prepared one-page summary or at least a topic list to distribute at the meeting. Every person should be allowed to make suggestions, express concerns, and ask questions. A good leader always treats suggestions in a positive and supportive manner, even if they are totally ridiculous and must be quietly ignored to prevent someone else from jumping on the bandwagon and painting MIS into the proverbial corner with no exit.

After several working days, the technical writer should contact at least one key user for additional discussions. A formal meeting, however, is not necessary and may even hinder progress! Usually a simple telephone call or informal chat in the company cafeteria will help the user remember those points missed during the meeting. Sometimes the best suggestions come from people sitting in a noisy cafeteria or standing around the coffee pot. Successful technical writers (and systems analysts) learn to use a combination of formality and informality—the trick is to decide which is appropriate.

Provide the users with a projected timetable for the entire project. The schedule should include checkpoints showing when user assistance is required, along with an estimate in employee-hours of their effort. It is unreasonable to ask a busy user (or anyone else) for help if one cannot provide the user with a rough estimate of the contribution needed.

Estimating dates is a combination of art, science, politics, and black magic. The writer should always stress verbally and on paper the tentative nature of the timetable, since many factors are beyond the writer's personal control. This is especially true when the author requires detailed assistance from other groups.

Report progress regularly. Users feel a personal interest and commitment only when they can see the project unfold before their eyes. The status report can also remind users of checkpoints drawing near when their assistance will be required. Good communication encourages cooperation and prevents those minor but annoying disagreements caused by the notorious "but I thought" syndrome. The motto of the technical writer who deals with users should be: No surprises.

As a result of following the foregoing steps, both the end users and the technical writer should feel a sense of accomplishment. Instead of having MIS personnel thrust a completed manual in their hands, the users will become true participants in the design, development, and packaging of their own manual. The results should be worth the effort.

5.5 WHO CONTROLS USER MANUALS?

The single document in MIS that causes the most confusion in determining ultimate responsibility is the user manual. Who makes the final decisions regarding the need to update, reprint, or modify a company's user manuals? Does MIS have the right to refuse or postpone a "legitimate" request? Can the accounting department require MIS to make corrections if the manual has errors or major omissions? What happens if the order entry manager says flatly, "It's not good enough. Do it over."

The obvious solution of asking higher management to arbitrate is not practical. Imagine the MIS director and accounting manager asking the senior vice president to judge each sentence in a documentation manual! Only in rare situations is it reasonable to proceed up the chain of command to settle documentation issues, and then *only* at the policy level.

Technical writers have discovered that unless an organization has a definite plan for documentation responsibilities, the burden often falls directly on them. *They* must negotiate, explain, and satisfy the users, while always being careful to accept reasonable suggestions from the people who actually use their products. In reality, technical writers often work for two areas, even when they report to MIS. A political ability to satisfy both their own managers, who often give them relative freedom, and their user base is critical to their success. Many technical writing specialists have more daily contact with users than with their own MIS colleagues or management!

The long-term solution is to develop a firm management policy regarding documentation responsibilities. Whatever the outcome, the agreement between MIS and the user departments should:

1. Give one group the responsibility for the mechanical aspects of documentation (i.e., creating, updating, and distributing).

2. Give another group the authority to accept or reject the documentation, with *a definite plan to make the documentation acceptable*. (Saying "we don't like it" is not good enough.)

3. Establish a user/MIS documentation committee to oversee documentation projects and recommend priorities.

4. Provide a process of periodic review by both users and MIS to examine user documentation and discuss problems before they become serious political issues.

If the technical writing staff reports to MIS, the MIS director must have final decision-making ability: likewise, if the staff works for the users, the appropriate user manager must have ultimate control. But successful technical writing is more than the ability to discover information and transfer it clearly to paper or CRT. It is the complex ability to negotiate, arbitrate, and satisfy people who come into a situation with differing goals. Human relations are often just as important as sentence structure!

5.6 DOCUMENTATION STANDARDS FOR USER MANUALS

Standardized user manuals—those with the same format, organization, and style—have several advantages:

1. With standardized user manuals, a user who transfers to another area is automatically familiar with the format of the new manual.

2. The technical writing staff becomes more proficient with one approach to documentation.
3. New technical writers do not (or at least should not) spend time searching for or developing another format.
4. Routine maintenance is often easier.

But in the real, day-to-day world of MIS, standards that appear great on paper do have disadvantages:

1. The single format may not fit all situations, and some user manuals may suffer in quality.
2. The technical writers may not develop their craft by "experimenting" with new styles and formats.
3. Some users may not like the standard and may push strongly for their own ideas.
4. Technical writers who do not like the standard (or who believe it does not fit their specific projects) may not do a thorough job.

Installations having years of experience with user manuals and their unique requirements may have enough knowledge to select one or even two formats that seem to fit most situations. By trial and error, they may have discovered formats that work and other formats that confuse more than they help. But other organizations that are relatively new to professional user documentation *should refrain from setting standards for the sake of having standards.* These shops need a certain amount of real-world experience (which includes both successes and failures) before they can make the jump to standardized user manuals.

5.7 SUMMARY OF KEY POINTS

☐ User manuals require extensive preparation before the writing begins. They must be planned like any other MIS project.
☐ User documentation can often be justified on the basis of reducing maintenance costs.

☐ Before contacting the user, the technical writer must learn everything possible from internal MIS sources.

☐ Even when everyone says, "There is no documentation!" there usually is. The author must play detective and find it!

☐ If allowed by company policy, the technical writer should use a tape recorder during interviews. It is difficult to accurately record a subject's every response by other means, especially when the interviewer is not familiar with the topic.

☐ Technical writers should constantly put themselves in the position of the user.

☐/ User manuals can be lively and even a little entertaining. Humor is justified if it does not interfere with communication.

☐ The writer should follow a logical plan for obtaining and holding user cooperation.

☐ A company needs a firm policy on user documentation that defines ultimate responsibilities and procedures for resolving disputes.

chapter **6**

User Manuals: The Mechanics

INTRODUCTION

This chapter shows how to prepare a successful user manual once the initial planning and research are complete. You should know the information in Chapter 5 before reading this material. This chapter explains the *macro-to-micro* or *general-to-specific* approach, whereby the author provides a logical framework before presenting detailed information. It describes the purpose and functions of the overview and explains the hierarchical approach to organizing user manuals. User documentation must be organized in accordance with the reader's job responsibilities rather than the structure of the MIS development or support team. Technical writers, systems analysts, users, and MIS managers can use these suggestions and guidelines to create efficient, well-organized user manuals.

Once the technical writer has evaluated the audience and gathered the necessary information, the second task is to plan the internals of the manual. Thorough planning is just as important to a writer as to a systems analyst, programmer, or manager. Indeed, many costly mistakes can be avoided if technical writers view their assignments as a series of projects, with all the requirements of true project management. *Good manuals simply do not just "happen"—they are planned.*

6.1 WRITING THE PREREQUISITE PAGE

What do the readers need *before* they open up the manual? Is there another document they should have read? Do they require a basic knowledge of accounting, retailing, or data processing? Many user manuals assume some level of prior experience or study, but few bother to clearly specify these requirements on a separate page. The manual should also repeat the prerequisites at critical points throughout the text, because some readers may ignore or forget the information given on the prerequisite page.

6.2 THE USER MANUAL OVERVIEW

Every user manual (and virtually any document over two pages long) needs an overview or summary that introduces the manual, describes the manual's purpose and intended audience, and prepares the reader for intelligent use of the manual. Starting to read a user manual without an overview is like jumping into a swimming pool filled with ice water —the effect is not very pleasant.

There is a very logical reason for always using an overview: a summary or overview fits into the macro-to-micro approach to education and training.

Users (and people in general) tend to understand a subject better when they proceed from the overall or macro level to the detail or micro level. *Details are often difficult to understand when the reader does not have a mental frame-*

work in which to organize those facts. One should not expect an accounting clerk to immediately jump into the proper use of transaction code 491 without knowing that transaction code 491 is one of seven accounts payable operations. People learn best when they appreciate the *relationships* among the details. In other words, both training and documentation should proceed from the general to the specific. The "big picture" approach is not a matter of courtesy, but simply a technique that improves the learning curve. In the 1980s, time is money.

The nature of an overview varies according to the situation. A manual designed to teach an order entry person the correct operating procedures for a minicomputer would need a relatively short overview. The documentation instructing the accounting staff how to use a new general ledger system would need a longer, more complex overview. In the latter case, the author could compose separate overviews for the various types of people who will be reading the manual. Accountants would need one approach, whereas accounting clerks might appreciate another style and a slightly different set of facts. *Each overview should be tailored to its audience.*

Many experienced writers—even those who are excellent at explaining details—shudder at the thought of writing an overview. Whereas the author of a system design document may correctly write the overview as the last step in the development process, the author of a user manual should create a skeleton or rough draft of the overview *before* starting the body of the manual. This exercise will help in focusing attention on the key points involved in creating a user manual. After the manual is complete, the author can revise the overview on the basis of the actual contents. Without this initial effort, the writer may forget or misinterpret key points, which could seriously damage the value of the project.

A good overview will answer the following questions:

- What is the purpose of the manual?
- Why do I need to read it?

- What exactly is the application (or system or product)?
- How will it help me do my job?
- What are the most important points to look for in this manual?
- Is there anything special I should understand about this application, such as its value to the company?
- How does this application fit into the organization?
- What are my duties in relation to this application?

The answers to these questions prepare the readers by giving them a friendly orientation to the task of reading the manual. Consider the following overview from an inventory control systems manual:

> This manual is for buyers, assistant buyers, and senior buyers who work with the inventory control system (ICS). The purpose of ICS is to monitor the movement of merchandise from the vendors to the warehouse to our retail stores in the Midwest. ICS automatically captures purchases, sales, returns, and adjustments, but depends on the buying staff to audit the daily and weekly error reports. File maintenance transactions must also be submitted to keep ICS correct. The buying staff analyzes the weekly stock status and other reports to spot trends and discover problem situations in each store and district. ICS is the only link between the warehouse and retail stores. It is vital to the entire vendor replenishment process, as well as to the accounting systems it feeds.

The overview tells the readers enough to understand the nature of the system and their general responsibilities. It also stresses the importance of ICS to the entire organization, which may improve the readers' motivation and job performance.

6.3 ORGANIZATION OF THE USER MANUAL

Although a logical organization or structure is vital to the success of any user manual, there is no single organizational scheme that will fit every situation. Technical writers should rely on their own experience and the examples around them to select the most effective structure for a specific project. What is suitable for one manual may be inappropriate for another, and significant changes to a system or product may justify an entirely new arrangement for the accompanying user manual.

The most common (and still quite effective) type of organization is the *hierarchical approach*. In general, the hierarchical approach divides the system into "logical" components that have a definite relationship to each other. That is, if a user manual analyzes the system or product in terms of four major topics, the user manual should have four chapters. Each chapter may then have individualized sections.

Although simple in theory, a good hierarchical approach is often difficult to implement because *there are multiple ways of breaking down any subject.* The author may view an application as consisting of logical sections A, B, and C, whereas the user may actually work with the system in terms of D, E, and F. The difference is subtle but important, because *user manuals should be designed to fit the hierarchy seen by the user, not that of the author.* An outline that is logical to one person may be nonsensical to another.

For example, many existing user manuals have separate chapters for transactions, reports, and internal processing. Is that approach logical? Yes, from the system designer's viewpoint, but not according to the orientation of the end consumer who actually uses the application. Members of the inventory control staff deal with "job responsibilities" rather than traditional MIS activities. For instance, "item add" transactions are part of the normal daily file maintenance procedure, and the manual therefore needs a chapter on daily file maintenance. Users demand documentation that follows *their* working habits, rather than an analysis of the system in technical terms. In fact, the best user manuals are often designed for individual job functions.

MIS often designs systems in pieces. One programmer creates the transactions and another develops the screen formats. But the typical user couldn't care less! The user sits down at a CRT to perform daily file maintenance, not to enter transactions.

A typical (but not totally efficient) user manual may follow the classical format:

1. Introduction
2. Transactions
3. Error reports
4. Standard reports
5. User-modifiable reports
6. Production cycles and options
7. Index

The preceding organization will eventually provide the needed information, but the users would describe the manual as a puzzle until they were thoroughly familar with the contents. The information is there, but it is not organized according to the users' normal activities.

A better structure is shown for a purchase order system:

1. Triggering purchase orders
2. Creating manual purchase orders
3. Paperwork disposition
4. Modifying the report formats
5. Error conditions with purchase orders
6. Relationship to open orders
7. Canceling or modifying purchase orders

This hierarchical table of contents does *not* separate the transactions created by Randy Record from either the artful screens developed by Carol Cathode or the aesthetically pleasing reports written by the plodding but ever faithful Charley Cobol. Instead, when clerks need to cancel a purchase order, they will go directly to section seven, which will tell them to use Randy's transaction 401 in Carol's INVMT screen and check faithful Charley's 801 hard-copy report. The manual has been designed for employees working with purchase orders, not for the MIS professionals who developed the system. The difference is subtle but important.

Even in departments with few employees, the gain in productivity is startling when user manuals are organized according to job function. The gains are even more impressive for large companies that make a sincere effort to organize user manuals around their daily activities. The hierarchical approach is logical as long as the author remembers to arrange the hierarchy according to users' needs.

6.4 INTERNALS OF THE USER MANUAL

The body of a user manual should proceed according to the macro-to-micro approach, and every chapter or major section should have an introductory paragraph that explains the purpose and organization of the chapter. Readers want to know *why* they should read that section and *how* it is arranged. A good author will try to *sell* the material to the customers, because getting people to actually use a manual is like trying to sell them vitamins: the introduction tells the readers why the product is good for them.

Descriptive titles can help readers quickly identify key portions of the text. In user manuals that are not written in narrative style, having a title for each paragraph may seem to interrupt the flow of the manual. But the convenience of quickly locating specific topics more than justifies the choppiness created by the frequent headings. Other manuals are written in narrative form, and for these the headings can be confined to major section breaks. A manual needed for quick reference should have more headings than a manual needed for general understanding. Again, defining the purpose of a user manual helps the writer select the correct number and placement of headings.

Authors must continually put themselves in the position of the end users of the application, system, or product. What do they need to know to accomplish their task? The truth may surprise even an experienced systems analyst. For example, an accounting clerk may need the procedure for turning on a CRT before entering data. A warehouse supervisor may not know instinctively how to power up the minicomputer, disk drive, and printer. Such details may be obvious to the analyst or technical writer, but not to the end user! The message is clear: think like a user, not as a DP professional. This shift of orientation must apply throughout the writing process.

Visualizing the situation from the users' point of view—especially that of the more naive or unsophisticated users—often requires the writer to spend significant amounts of time working with the users in their environment. There is no substitute for visiting a department, taking a detailed tour, and then simply wandering around the area informally chatting with people. This rule applies not only to the information-gathering stage, but to the stage at which the author is busy creating the manual! In addition to picking up valuable information, technical writers can eventually enable themselves to judge the level of data-processing sophistication of their future customers. They can also learn more about the problems, feelings, and frustration levels of their audience.

When creating the manual, the author should attempt to put error codes, warning messages, and error recovery procedures where they will be needed—*if* the user is following detailed instructions. For example, a programmer using a data-base host language interface "open" routine may get a program termination with a code A456. A technical writer could easily document the error codes in the appendix (and probably will), but should at least mention the most common "open errors" in the section describing the "open" instruction. In many real-life situations, the typical mistakes, errors, and omissions can be accurately predicted, and if the technical writer can anticipate the most likely mistakes, this will help increase user productivity. Imagine the programmer seeing the explanation for A456 on the same page as the "open" command! There is no need to shift mental gears and locate the error in the appendix, and the immediate gain in productivity is significant—not just because of the time saved, but because the user did not have to switch to a different mental orientation or mind set.

The audience for a technical manual often consists of both experienced and naive users, and the writer has the obvious problem of trying to satisfy both groups. If the author has decided to create one manual for both groups (a common practice because of time constraints), the sophisticated user must be able to skip over unnecessary information. Helpful statements may be "If you know how to operate a 3270 CRT, go to paragraph C4" or "If you understand the difference between LIFO and FIFO, go to section B in the next chapter." It is also reasonable to change the writing style in paragraphs or sections that are directed toward naive users. For example, a reader who has never worked a 3270 CRT may need a detailed, forgiving, and simplified writing style. The section explaining LIFO and FIFO need not assume a knowledge of accounting and can be written for someone who has never taken an accounting course.

Both technical MIS manuals and business system manuals often depend on information in other documents. Therefore, the technical writer should carefully list references to other manuals or documents. For example, when confused by a statement in the inventory control manual, a retail company buyer may not automatically turn to the order processing manual for an explanation of "retail price rounding." The inventory manual should direct the buyer to the appropriate other documents. The author should never be afraid to insult readers by explicitly listing other references or places to go for assistance. This practice is one trademark of good user documentation.

Manuals are more interesting and effective when the author uses terms familiar to the user. To an MIS professional, the physical location where customer orders are processed is simply one desk out of ten in the order entry department on the fifth floor. But to anyone in the section, that special desk is called "order control." The employees may refer to it as "OC" or by some more colorful term. Manuals should contain the users' own buzzwords and colloquial expressions, if they have stood the test of time. (One would not include casual expressions used only by one individual.) The manual will then seem more natural or custom-designed and therefore more relevant to the reader.

What happens when the manual cannot explain a particular problem or address a complex issue? Users are further puzzled when the manual does not provide them with specific instructions. The documentation should direct them to the next logical place for assistance, whether it is another manual, the MIS systems group, or the vendor. *It is unreasonable to expect a user manual to solve all problems,* and the body of the text should contain frequent comments about outside assistance. If the trial balance report is incorrect because an account number is rejected, should the accounting clerk call MIS or talk to the supervisor? If the manual directs the clerk to call MIS, is it necessary to first call Operations, Systems and Programming, Quality Assurance, the Office of the Director, or the MIS secretary the clerk had lunch with last week? Problems will develop in any computer system, and the manual should honestly tell the user how to resolve those problems.

When writing the body of the documentation, the author should maintain a relatively consistent format, style, vocabulary, and writing technique. The exception is when the author provides separate sections for naive and sophisticated users. But within a section or chapter written for the same generic audience, the author should maintain consistency. If several technical writers and systems analysts join forces to create a large manual, the manager or senior writer should make sure that the writers have a similar or at least complementary style. A manual that has widely differing styles will frustrate many readers.

The index is the final cross-reference feature and should be developed with great care. With a complete index, users can go directly to specific areas of interest. Often a user who is already familiar with the system can evaluate the completeness of an index and suggest improvements. *The index should be as carefully prepared as the overview or introduction.*

6.5 FIELD TESTING THE MANUAL

Inexperienced technical writers deliver a completed user manual to the accounting department and say, "I hope you like it!" This is not an appropriate business statement. The users should have been examining, criticizing, and approving the manual as it was being developed. If the users have not participated in the development, they can at least approve the manual on a chapter-by-chapter basis.

But even with the closest cooperation between MIS and the users, one final step remains. Just as computer programs must be tested before production, user manuals must be field tested with the same care given to a new application system. A program, system, or electronic device rarely works perfectly the first time, and user manuals are no different. All parties involved, including MIS and the user group management, must understand clearly that even if the manual is "accepted" by the users, a field test is absolutely necessary. The project is not complete until the field test has uncovered the inevitable errors and omissions.

The concept of *acceptance* is often misunderstood in MIS, and by those who still believe that a strict dichotomy exists between nonacceptance and acceptance of a system, application, or product. For most complex MIS products—such as user manuals—this theory is false. Users cannot possibly verify every feature in a complex or sophisticated application, and neither can they verify every section, sentence, and word in a user manual. The long-awaited words "I accept" should be changed to "I tentatively accept," and field testing should be an integral part of that acceptance procedure.

Field testing requires cooperation between MIS and several volunteer users. In some cases, the manual is the first documentation they have seen, and therefore the entire process of using documentation is new. But even new users can still provide helpful comments and suggestions. The friendly interaction between technical writer and user helps clarify points that were not properly understood.

The volunteers should understand that their role is to provide constructive feedback to the technical writer, and that the field-testing phase is not the time to suggest a complete rewrite or major changes to the manual. Rather, users can point out missing pieces, suggest changes in wording or terminology, or propose a rearrangement of the material. The field-testing phase should last as long as the production cycles involved in the application. That is, if the user manual describes a system that has daily, weekly, and monthly cycles, the field-testing phase should carry through into the next month's processing. Of course, one cannot always carry this guideline to its logical conclusion. A chapter on year-end processing may need to wait until the following year end for evaluation, although the rest of the manual can certainly be tested, modified, and approved. With most production business systems, a five- to six-week testing phase is adequate, if the users are truly working with the manual and providing regular feedback.

6.6 REVISIONS

Documentation must evolve along with application system enhancements, hardware improvements, and personnel changes. Even with those rare business systems that are perfectly stable, as the users gain more experience with both the product and the manual, they will find areas that need improvement. MIS needs an easy-to-use procedure that will allow all interested parties to suggest, monitor, and implement changes to completed user manuals. The procedure can involve a special form, a memo to the technical writing staff or application support group, or a joint MIS/user committee that oversees user documentation.

Manuals need a "change page" that lists the purpose and nature of the latest modifications. For example, revision

3.0 of an accounts payable manual might list the following changes:

- Added new purchases reconciliation subsystem
- Upgraded edit screen error messages
- Deleted obsolete reports 401, 402, and 403

Giving people a new manual is like giving them a new car, desk, or office. Their first reaction is: What's different from the old one? By documenting the changes, the technical writer will save the users the time and frustration involved in having to discover the differences for themselves. When the frustration level increases beyond a certain limit, some users have been known to ignore the revised document and use the old manual!

6.7 SPECIAL CONSIDERATIONS FOR ONLINE USER MANUALS

User documentation accessed through a CRT has several unique requirements. Simply loading paper-oriented documentation into an online library is only the first step: the material should be revised to fit the needs of a viewer using a CRT.

Visible page size is an important factor. With hard-copy documentation, the user can easily flip back to see the start of a thought or topic on the previous page. Sentences and paragraphs frequently spread across two pages, with little impact on the reader. We accept without question the need to occasionally span a page of a report, document, or book. But when a CRT replaces the hard copy, the user no longer has that luxury. It is possible to page back to the previous screen, but there is often a delay of as much as several seconds, and this time lag makes the process inefficient. Even a one-second delay is often enough to break a user's mental concentration. With online documentation, each screen should be a separate, easily understandable entity. The author should write documentation on a screen-by-screen basis as if the user could not return to the previous screen. This guideline (which is obviously false) will help the writer compose each screen as a "whole."

The second requirement is that every CRT document screen should tell users exactly where they have been and where they are going. Traditionally, online systems use the standard procedures "Press PF1 to Continue" and "Press PF2 to Return." This is not acceptable for online documentation. *Users must know where they have come from and where they are going.* A better message would be "Press PF1 to See Screen 3-of-4 of Purchase Order Cancellation" and "Press PF2 to Return to Purchase Order Main Menu." The prompt should change with every screen to tell users their exact location.

6.8 SUMMARY OF KEY POINTS

☐ The overview helps the readers understand why they should study the manual and how the subject fits in with their job responsibilities.

☐ The overview should be designed specifically for the audience. If there are two or more target groups, there must be two or more overviews.

☐ The hierarchical approach to user manual organization works well if the author uses the hierarchy of the user's job functions. Manuals should be organized in accordance with user responsibilities, not according to the organization of the MIS development or support team.

☐ Frequent descriptive titles should be used in the body of the manual, even if they seem to make the material choppy.

☐ Each page of online documentation should be a complete "thought" and should not run over to the next screen, even if some pages are short.

☐ Each online screen must tell users exactly where they are according to the user manual organization.

chapter **7**

Data Center Documentation

INTRODUCTION

A data center depends on documentation to manage computer processing, resolve the inevitable problems, and satisfy basic reporting needs. Many mistakes and production errors are directly or indirectly caused by poor-quality written communication. This chapter provides sample run instructions and problem-reporting logs along with the correct procedures for using them. It describes special procedures documentation and master system documentation books, both of which help control even the most complex environment. Data center managers and technical writers can use these sample forms and instructions to quickly improve both daily and long-term operations.

Today's large data centers are not simple "black boxes"

that automatically accept data through one door and spew reports through another—some data centers even function as separate business units. Most MIS departments require a large number of operations and support personnel, and these staff members communicate through specialized forms and reports. If their written communication is not efficient, productivity decreases and problems increase. A well-managed data center has precise, exact, and concise communication both internally and externally. More important, *data center documents should always reflect desired management policies.*

7.1 RUN SHEETS

A technical writer or manager investigating the complex subject of run sheets should appreciate the historical problems—and the opinions—associated with these documents. Run sheets are known by many names in each operations department, most of which should not be repeated around young children. Rarely does one find an organization that has seriously attempted to create a useful operational run sheet that actually helps operators rather than hinders them. One obvious reason for this lack of progress is tradition. Data center managers may be comfortable with an old, archaic formate everyone knows is virtually useless, and the managers may be reluctant to change. Perhaps they fear that a new format might be worse than the old one!

Run documentation invariably seems to be incorrect, confusing, and contradictory. When a production problem arises, existing documentation seldom helps. Operators complain so much that their suggestions are ignored or disregarded. Some operators revert to the time-honored practice of calling another operator or the supporting programmer. If that fails, they may fall back on the even older practice of trying solutions at random. Eventually, one may seem to work, or the problem may become so confused that they must turn the entire fiasco over to the programming staff.

But operational run instructions *can* be clear, useful, and informative if MIS management is willing to make good documentation a departmental priority. Even the best run sheets will never win a prize for creative writing, but they can indeed serve as the "final authority" for job setup, processing, and problem resolution. Run sheets can be useful, but they require hard work and logical thinking.

The first step in creating good documentation is to define the basic purpose of operational run sheets (besides satisfying the requirements of the internal or external auditors). Run sheets should:

- Help in job scheduling.
- Inform the tape library which tapes need to be staged, and which will be created.
- Tell the operators which demountable units are needed during the job.
- Give the operations staff enough information to handle restarts and reruns without asking for assistance from either programming or technical support personnel.

Operational run instructions that go beyond these four basic needs may have too much information. For example, some managers demand that run instructions list all work files and their space allocations for "information purposes." This increases both the length and the complexity of run sheets, and the details are seldom accurate. Management must strike a balance between what is nice to have and the amount of work needed to maintain the extra data fields. For example, the hardware analyst may demand run sheets that list the current space allocations of work files, but the burden of updating such information may cause the staff to ignore run sheets altogether. *Operational documentation should be designed with the goal of minimum effort in mind.* That is, the team designing the run sheets should verify that all proposed information is worth the effort. If Charley Channel, the hardware analyst, wants to see specific unit and device information for each job, how much effort will this require? How often does the information change? Does anyone else really need those data? More important, do the people who actually use the run sheets on a daily basis need the unit and device information? If the answer is no, the information should not be on the form. Let Charley track his own data.

Run sheets should be stored in a manner that allows for easy and quick changes. The writer should avoid the typewriter for the same reasons that analysts creating user documentation and system design documents avoid the typewriter. One of the best devices for developing and storing operational instructions is a word processor or online text-editing system. The requirements for an optimum system are described in the Appendix. Whatever the medium, run sheets should be relatively easy to modify by computer operators and tape librarians. Although programmers will make changes as they install enhancements and new features, update control should not be left exclusively with the systems and programming personnel. Rather, in an ideal situation (with reasonable cooperation among departments), all users should have the ability to update, correct, and modify operational instructions as needed.

Although groups should share the responsibility for updating run documentation, one individual or section must have final responsibility for verifying the final product and for arbitrating the inevitable disputes. Normally, this is done by the operations director, but it could easily be done by the programming or technical support manager. This person will need a mechanism to track which individuals made changes to the run sheets and whether these persons distributed the revisions to everyone who keeps hard-copy listings. An alternative is to allow only one person to make the physical changes and control the distribution, but this approach must be simple and direct—if the change procedure is cumbersome, some employees will not make the effort, and the run sheets will never be maintained. Perhaps the best policy is to try unrestricted access and, if serious control problems develop, appoint one person as "run sheet czar" to take charge of all operational documentation. In high-pressure data-processing environments, this last policy may be the only one that works.

Like other forms of documentation, run sheets need to be periodically revised as the hardware and software environment changes, and as employees become familiar with the value of useful documentation. Continual use of documentation is not only enlightening but educational; as employees gain experience, they will make positive suggestions for improvement. Of course, management must insist that each change is justified and is not merely a whim.

Another problem with run sheets is that traditional formats seldom allow free-form expressions. To a certain extent, every production job is slightly different and requires special instructions regarding restart, rerun, timing, or job resource allocation. Every form needs space for "overflow" information. For example, if the rerun procedure requires more space than the "Rerun" section allows, the form should have considerable additional space for "Comments." The "Comments" area can be used for many things.

Run sheet formats differ for each operating system; Figure 7.1 illustrates run documentation for an IBM OS installation. Any additional software used by the operations department will affect the information on the form. A "Restart Management System," for example, which automatically resets generation data groups and scratches unneeded data sets will reduce the amount of restart information.

Should IBM OS restart and rerun instructions reside in the run documentation or should they be listed as comments in the JCL (job control language) procedure? The arguments are strong on both sides of the issue, but a number of operations managers feel that step-level restart instructions should be stated in the procedure rather than in separate documentation. If a job in an IBM OS installation abends, the shift supervisor, support technician, or operator will usually examine the hard-copy (or online) JCL listing. Therefore, it is more efficient for most OS shops to keep their step-level restart instructions in the procedure. For rerun documentation, the opposite logic applies. If a job

Job Name: _____ Description: _____

Date Revised: _____ By: _____

System: _____

Alternate Names for Job: _____

Purpose of Job: _____

_____

_____

A.   *SETUP AND TIMING*

A.1. Prerequisite job(s): _____

_____

_____

A.2. Following job(s): _____

_____

A.3. Frequency: Nightly   ____ Daily   ____

                     Monthly   ____ Weekly   ____

                     Biweekly   ____ Quarterly ____

                     On request   ____ Yearly   ____

                     Internal need ____ Other   ____

If "on request" or "internal need," who provides the decision? How does the information get trans-ᐧ mitted to the operator?

_____

_____

Figure 7.1 Run Sheet for an IBM OS Installation

A.4. Normal processing time (in hours): _____

Maximum: _____

A.5. Normal run schedule: Start time _____

Stop time _____

A.6. Special requirements (not tape or disk): _____

_____

_____

A.7. Input tapes from other jobs?

Yes _____   No _____

DSN	FROM JOB	FROM STEP	TO STEP	DISPOSITION	
_____	_____	_____	_____	Scratch ___	Save ___
_____	_____	_____	_____	Scratch ___	Save ___
_____	_____	_____	_____	Scratch ___	Save ___
_____	_____	_____	_____	Scratch ___	Save ___
_____	_____	_____	_____	Scratch ___	Save ___

A.8. How many scratch tapes are needed? _____

A.9. Any removable disk devices needed?

Yes _____   No _____

If yes, which packs? _____ _____ _____ _____

A.10. Any other special setup requirements?

_____

_____

_____

Figure 7.1 Run Sheet For an IBM OS Installation *(Continued)*

B. *PROCESSING*

B.1. Tape and disk:

STEP	DESCRIPTION	INPUT TAPE, DSN OR REMOVABLE DISK	OUTPUT TAPE, DSN OR REMOVABLE DISK
‾‾	‾‾‾‾‾‾‾	‾‾‾‾‾	‾‾‾‾‾
‾‾	‾‾‾‾‾‾‾	‾‾‾‾‾	‾‾‾‾‾
‾‾	‾‾‾‾‾‾‾	‾‾‾‾‾	‾‾‾‾‾
‾‾	‾‾‾‾‾‾‾	‾‾‾‾‾	‾‾‾‾‾
‾‾	‾‾‾‾‾‾‾	‾‾‾‾‾	‾‾‾‾‾
‾‾	‾‾‾‾‾‾‾	‾‾‾‾‾	‾‾‾‾‾
‾‾	‾‾‾‾‾‾‾	‾‾‾‾‾	‾‾‾‾‾
‾‾	‾‾‾‾‾‾‾	‾‾‾‾‾	‾‾‾‾‾
‾‾	‾‾‾‾‾‾‾	‾‾‾‾‾	‾‾‾‾‾
‾‾	‾‾‾‾‾‾‾	‾‾‾‾‾	‾‾‾‾‾

B.2. Control cards?   Yes _____   No _____

If yes, describe format: _____

_____

_____

Who prepares the control card?

Shift supervisor _____   Data entry _____

User _____   Operator _____   Other _____

Figure 7.1 *(Continued)*

Who answers questions about the control card?

_____

Where are control cards placed? _____

_____

Disposition of cards: Scrap ____

Save in deck ____   Other ____

B.3. Console messages and replies:

	RESPONSE
MESSAGE	**("I" if Information Only)**
_____	_____
_____	_____
_____	_____
_____	_____
_____	_____
_____	_____
_____	_____
_____	_____

B.4. Any special processing requirements not yet listed?

_____

_____

_____

_____

_____

Figure 7.1 Run Sheet for an IBM OS Installation *(Continued)*

C.   *RERUN INSTRUCTIONS*

Rerun procedures are often based on a specific problem. Please locate the cause and use the corresponding procedure.

C.1. Why do you need to do a rerun?

REASON	SEE PROCEDURE

C.2. Specific procedures:

NUMBER	ACTION

Figure 7.1 (*Continued*)

C.3. General comments on reruns (cautions, potential problems, etc.):

_____

_____

_____

_____

_____

_____

_____

_____

D.   *ADDITIONAL INFORMATION*

D.1. Report distribution: Priority   ____

                                  Normal   ____

                                  Overnight   ____

                                  Standard paper ____

                                  Form number   ____

                                  Fiche   ____

                                  Number of parts (if not 1) ____

Original to: _____

Copy 1 to: _____

Copy 2 to: _____

Copy 3 to: _____

Copy 4 to: _____

Figure 7.1   Run Sheet for an IBM OS Installation *(Continued)*

D.2. User notification?   Yes ____   No ____

Contact: Name _____

Office _____   Area _____

Phone _____

Alternate phone _____

Notify immediately?

Yes ____   No ____

Notify via _____

D.3. Balance procedures?   Yes ____   No ____

Describe: _____

_____

_____

_____

_____

If out-of-balance, describe action: _____

_____

_____

_____

D.4. Quality control:

Check JCL listing?   Yes ____   No ____

Condition code check: _____

Sort counts: _____

Record counts: _____

Figure 7.1 (*Continued*)

Check anything else? _____

_____

_____

JCL disposition: Normal ____ or send to ____

_____

D.5. If this job abends and cannot be restarted, what action should be taken?

_____ Save until next working day and send to Systems.

_____ Call Systems immediately.

_____ Call on-duty analyst for that application immediately.

_____ Call Systems in the morning.

_____ Postpone the following jobs until resolved:

_____ _____ _____ _____

What will the impact be if this job is not completed on schedule?

_____

_____

D.6. If the job is not completed during the shift, who else should be called?

_____

_____

_____

When? Immediately ____ Morning ____

Next working day ____

Figure 7.1 Run Sheet for an IBM OS Installation *(Continued)*

is complete and must be rerun, the operations staff should go to a separate set of instructions (such as run sheets). Rerun procedures can also be more complicated than restarts and may require long narrative explanations. Comments are excellent documentation to include in the JCL listing, but this is no place for long narration!

Whatever the decision, all jobs in the shop should follow the same standard approach. For example, all step-level restart instructions should be in the procedure, and all rerun information should be in the run sheets. Without standards, the operations staff members will be confused when they come to the normal restart/rerun questions that always arise, and the mistakes will be painful.

Operational documentation such as run sheets should be designed as an extension of management policy, just as system design documents and feasibility statements should carry out management directives. By using carefully engineered formats, MIS management can answer those nagging, troublesome questions, such as: Who do I call when something goes wrong? These puzzles should be answered in writing as the result of a thoughtful evaluation rather than at 2:00 AM during a busy month-end weekend.

The same form can also be used by both the tape library and the forms distribution section. Some installations utilize separate forms for Operations, the tape library, and Data Control, which becomes confusing and eventually causes duplicate information.

A good run sheet is a reference tool rather than a narrative document. The difference is subtle but still important. The tape librarian who needs setup information should know that section A will always provide tape information. The computer operator should know that section C always contains rerun information. When tape information is needed, the computer operator should also know where it is located *on the same form.*

Well-designed run sheets also acknowledge that reruns are a fact of life in MIS departments, and that *good documentation prepared before the rerun helps reduce serious problems.* If a job is important enough to require a computer, it is important enough to deserve advance planning for rerun purposes.

7.1.1 Explanation of the Sample Run Sheet

The following comments help explain the philosophy behind selected entries of the sample run sheet Figure 7.1. A form is more useful when all those concerned understand the purpose!

Initial information. Every document (including a run sheet) should have a "date revised" field. When changes are made to the run sheet, the initials of the person making the changes should be listed along with the change date.

The "alternate names for job" space prevents misunderstanding, because installations typically have more than one informal name for the same job. The jobstream that creates purchase orders may be called "PO Generate," "Purchase Orders," "Process PO Master," "PO4440," or simply "PO." All these names refer to the same job, but they are used by different people in different departments. Since alternate names cannot be avoided, the run sheet should recognize their existence.

The "purpose of job" entry summarizes the job and its relationship to the application system.

Section A: Setup and Timing. Question 3 reduces the mystery concerning those production jobs that are run on specific request or because they simply "must be run." The frequency of a surprisingly large number of production jobs is determined by someone's instinct rather than specific instructions.

Section B: Processing. Question 2 defines the origin, use, and disposition of control cards that are used by older production systems. Too often computer operators simply throw away the cards because they are not sure what to do with them, or merely leave them in the deck.

Section C: Rerun Instructions. The first question requires the operator or supervisor to define the reason for a rerun, because selecting the best rerun procedure may depend on the cause of the problem. If job Y abends because of a bad tape from job X, the operator may follow a different procedure than that used for a program error. Incorrect or inappropriate rerun procedures are a curse in many computer centers, and most of those periodic disasters can be avoided by careful planning before the inevitable problems arise.

Section D: Additional Information. Quality control checks and balance information are vital to many production jobs and should be documented directly in the run sheets. Computer operators and control clerks need definite instructions on handling errors: Who do they contact? Can they continue? What are the effects? These questions should be discussed and settled in a quiet conference room during the day so that a slightly panicky computer operator will not make a best guess at 2:00 AM. Murphy has consistently proven that slightly panicky computer operators at 2:00 AM are not the best decision makers.

7.2 PROBLEM-REPORTING LOGS

Whenever any significant problem occurs in a large, multi-CPU data center or even in a small minicomputer operation, the response should be the same: the problem should be efficiently logged, evaluated, and resolved with a minimum of human time and computer expense. That scenario does not always happen. Some data centers are viewed as the weak spot in the chain that links the customer to the finished product. And efforts to strengthen that weak link are frustrating. Even experienced MIS managers frequently describe the computer room as a mysterious black box that devours phone calls. Memos and verbal questions often receive the same response: No, I don't know where it stands.

Formalized problem-reporting logs, combined with a firm commitment to always use them, will help reduce that confusion. When a problem appears that cannot be solved immediately, the problem log will start that tracking process and make sure that the staff moves toward an eventual resolution. People can always say "I didn't know about that" or "I forgot," but those excuses become very shaky when the problem has been immediately logged on paper or into an online text editor. When excuses start to melt away, efficiency quickly rises!

Implementing a problem log procedure (sometimes called an *interrupt* or *situation* procedure) requires careful planning by the operations staff. MIS management must insist that all areas of the organization faithfully follow the problem log reporting procedure—the concept is useless unless people let the system work!

The four keys to a practical and successful system are:

1. Make the form easy to use, with checkmarks, circles, or single-key entries replacing most of the writing. Busy operations personnel do have time for long sessions with a with a CRT or a pencil when disaster strikes. If the form requires too much time, they will usually handle the problem and fill out the form after the fact. This common but unfortunate practice reduces the value of any problem-tracking system. The form should be used *as the problem is happening.*

2. Teach the staff to *logically* evaluate the priority of each problem, which includes an immediate estimate of the possible implications. The person taking the call or investigating the potential problem should have enough experience to judge the seriousness of the problem. Deciding severity by assessing user reactions is always dangerous, since one user may complain bitterly about an incorrect figure of little importance, whereas another user may casually mention an incorrect week number in a heading line, indicating that the entire weekend processing is wrong.

3. Create a workable but efficient paper flow. A computer operator will not willingly stand at a copy machine making seventeen copies of a problem log. Nor will the operator chase three managers for their signatures every time a problem occurs. The work flow must be simple and fast.

4. Encourage the entire MIS department to view problem logs as helpful tools rather than another paperwork curse, or as a document that points the accusing finger of guilt. Because of poor management practices, problem-reporting logs can cause more trouble than the original event when they are used to fix blame.

7.2.1 When to Use a Problem Log

Problem logs are most useful when everyone in the organization understands when they are needed and when they are quite literally a waste of time. Making that distinction is often difficult! Management should create a policy document listing specific examples of situations in which a problem log is needed and other situations in which its use is not justified. Certainly the MIS management team does not want to have every phone call or request that comes into a data center or computer room entered in the problem log, but only those interrupts that are significant. The term "significant" is virtually impossible to define, since it varies with the environment and the degree of control that management wishes to exert. The best guidelines—or perhaps the only ones that actually work—are those that include realistic, understandable examples.

7.2.2 Explanation of the Sample
Problem-Reporting Log

Figure 7.2 illustrates a problem log designed for an IBM OS data center with online and overnight batch applications. One form can handle both types of situations, although online interrupts are qualitatively different than overnight batch problems. Although this suggested format does have most of the information needed for many organizations, a problem-reporting log usually needs some degree of customization.

The entries in a problem log are usually self-explanatory if the designer has used descriptive titles that are meaningful to the operations staff. Of course, some instructions are still needed. As with all other forms, a problem log must be tested by the actual users in a production-like situation. This test determines the level of documentation needed. The following explanation will give MIS management a basic understanding of the reasoning behind some of the entries and sections in Figure 7.2.

Problem logs are often corrected after the fact, or as new information is developed. The analyst or manager can

Number: ____

Date: _____

Logged by: _____

Time: _____

Original: _____

Corrected copy: _____ Refers to no.: _____

Date corrected: _____ Corrected by: _____

Section: _____

| **SOURCE** | | **PRIORITY** |

Job ____ Scheduled ____ Informational ____

User ____ Nonscheduled ____ Normal ____

Internal ____ Serious ____

MIS info. ____ Critical ____

Route copies to:

Software: ____

Data control: ____ (DC gets original back.)

Applications: ____

User: Finance ____ Order control ____ Dist ____

Administration ____ Warehouse ____

Sales ____ Planning ____ Other ____

Note: Send copy of all serious and critical problems to MIS director.

Figure 7.2 Problem-Reporting Log

A. *GENERAL INFORMATION*

Name: _____ Abended? _____ Abend code(s): _____

Messages: _____

Action taken: _____

_____

_____

Probable cause: _____

_____

Application _____ Disk _____ Tape _____ Operator _____

User input _____ Documentation _____ JCL _____

Unknown _____ Other _____

Final cause: Determined by _____

Date _____ Section _____

Application _____ Disk _____ Tape _____ Operator _____

User input _____ Documentation _____ JCL _____

Unknown _____ Other _____

Critical path problem? _____

Restart time: _____ Restart date, if different: _____

Assistance required during restart?

From whom? _____ On-site _____

Time notified _____ Notified by _____ Arrived _____

Restart documentation correct? _____ If not, what was
wrong?

_____

Figure 7.2 *(Continued)*

Comments: _____

_____

_____

B.   *ONLINE APPLICATION*

Task name: _____ System: _____

Abend code: _____ Console message: _____

Date base abend flag set? ____

    If yes, what time did you start checkpoint recovery?

    What time was recovery complete? _____

    What time was task restarted? _____

Probable cause: Application ____ Disk ____

                Operator cancel ____

                File lockout ____ Loop ____ Data ____

                Unknown ____ Other ____

Final cause: Determined by _____

                Date _____ Time _____

                Application ____ Disk ____

                Operator cancel ____

                File lockout ____ Loop ____ Data ____

                Unknown ____ Other ____

Comments: _____

_____

_____

Figure 7.2 Problem-Reporting Log *(Continued)*

C.   *OTHER INFORMATION*

Job ran incorrectly,
Rerun needed _____ but no rerun needed _____

Output from job no. _____ lost _____

Printer manfunction,   Missing
   several jobs lost _____ tape _____

Tape drive no. _____

   Malfunction _____

   Notified vendor at _____

   Responded at _____

   Fixed at _____

Disk drive no. _____

   Malfunction _____

   Notified vendor at _____

   Responded at _____

   Fixed at _____

   Additional recovery needed? _____

UPS problem _____

   Condition _____

   Called service at _____

   Responded at _____

   Cause _____

   Fixed at _____

   How long was CPU down? _____

Figure 7.2 *(Continued)*

Communication problem _____

    Line no. _____

    Error code _____

    Notified vendor at _____

    Fixed at _____

    Explanation _____

    _____

    _____

Incorrect report _____

    Notified by _____

    Investigated by _____

    System _____

    Possible error in job no. _____

    Action taken _____

    _____

    _____

Other problems _____

_____

_____

_____

_____

_____

Figure 7.2 Problem-Reporting Log *(Continued)*

then check the "corrected copy" entry, fill in the "logged by" space, and note which original problem the revision applies to. A common (and quite justified) complaint among operations managers is that incorrect problem logs are never revised. For example, if a production abend is initially charged to a program error, but further research points to a transient hardware problem on a tape drive, the real cause of the problem may never be communicated. If a problem is important enough to need a written problem log, it is important enough to be updated with correct information. The purpose is never to place blame, but simply to communicate the facts. The operations staff should know that a transient hardware error caused job number 456 to abend last night so that they can watch for additional problems on that tape drive or controller.

Many problem logs are for information only, and employees should not waste valuable time reading about those frequent but annoying troubles that routinely arise in a busy data center. They should, however, know that the problems occurred. The operator who checks the entry should be reasonably sure that no one else in the organization needs to follow up on the problem, although it is still an individual manager's responsibility to audit any "suspicious-looking" problem log.

An interrupt is "serious" when a production jobstream is holding up subsequent jobs or may not meet its assigned completion schedule. A problem is "critical" when the major production schedule in the shop will not be met unless the problem is resolved immediately. An example is a disk failure that destroys an important data base, requiring quick action in restoring the file, reprocessing updates, notifying the users, and restarting the online tasks. Another example is when a bad input tape in a job stops the entire overnight critical path, and the tape cannot be recreated through normal means. Unless the problem is resolved, all overnight critical path jobs will be held up, which will hold up the online day. In a banking environment, this type of situation could be devastating.

The originator of a problem log should determine who

else needs to be aware of the interrupt. Not everyone in a large organization should be notified of all interrupts, so a single individual (either the originator or an "interrupt controller") must decide who gets copies of each interrupt form. However, there must be one physical location (such as a common file cabinet) where a copy of each interrupt is kept, so that any authorized person can research previous problems.

When an interrupt or problem first occurs, the operator may not have enough information to pinpoint the probable cause. Later, however, as the job is restarted or as more is learned about the situation, the operator may form a different opinion. The "final cause" entry is used only when the operator, originator, or some other staff member discovers the true nature of the problem.

Operators occasionally discover that restart documentation is nonexistent or incorrect, and the problem log allows them to note that condition.

Since online processing varies according to the hardware, software, and systems in use, the problem log suggested for an online type of interrupt in Figure 7.2 must be revised to match a specific environment.

Since the number of possible interruptions in a data center is almost infinite, the "Other Information" section lists only a few of the more common possibilities. Again, the format allows the originator to use check marks or a single stroke on the keyboard rather than words or even phrases. By reducing the manual effort, this approach encourages the operations staff (and others) to fill out problem logs faithfully and accurately.

7.3 SPECIAL PROCEDURES DOCUMENTATION

Run sheets and other problem logs are not enough to run a data center, because many serious real-life situations cannot be traced to particular production jobs or specific problems. For example, a disk head crash that destroyed several critical permanent files will require a detailed recovery plan and a realignment of the subsequent production schedule. The implications are both serious and complicated. The only thing worse than a head crash is a hastily created recovery plan that restores the wrong files at the wrong time! A once-a-year event such as warehouse physical inventory will need detailed system flowcharts so that all involved know their specific responsibilities. Both of these examples are usually looked on as potential crises by operations managers, because they are invariably the source of irritating and continuing problems. But the event itself does not cause the irritation; rather, it is caused by the lack of planning and lack of documentation. For many companies, taking a once-a-year physical inventory is like a bad dream, but taking a physical inventory when the important players are confused is a nightmare.

To reduce this confusion, managers and other employees should predict "worst case scenarios" and prepare for those situations by producing careful documentation. The act of creating documentation forces employees to prepare for all eventualities. Too often the operational management team looks at planning as an activity restricted to yearly budgets and future hardware upgrades, whereas good planning covers all areas of data center activity.

Perhaps the lack of forethought is caused by a reluctance to envision the worst. No one likes to anticipate a head crash on the most important pack in the shop, and no one cares to think about what *can* go wrong during a yearly physical inventory. Optimists are fun to be around, but one or two pessimists are valuable during the planning process.

One of several outputs resulting from this "enlightened preparation" approach is a manual called *special procedures documentation,* which contains solutions and answers for those generalized problems that may occur in the future. This collection of information will become just as important to the data center as the book containing detailed run sheets, and it should be treated with equal respect.

7.3.1 Examples of Special Procedures Topics

The subjects in a special procedures manual depend on the activities of the particular shop. Some common events that can be included are:

1. Disk crashes on the permanent production packs.
   a. What recovery method is possible?
   b. How many application systems are involved?
   c. What departments should be notified?
   d. What other systems are not involved and can be run normally?
2. Once- or twice-a-year applications that need coordination within the data center or with user departments.
   a. Who schedules the activity?
   b. How does the data center fit into the picture?
   c. What planning meetings are necessary, and who should attend?
   d. What department or section has the "experts" who can provide additional information?
   e. Does the data center need any special staffing to handle this event?
   f. Should the tape library or technical support be involved?
3. Situations in which the entire overnight or weekend batch integrated systems must be rerun.
   a. Who or what group should coordinate the effort?
   b. What reports and/or files are wrong and should be discarded?
   c. What should the users be told? Can they use any information from the incorrect reports?
   d. What unusual problems can be anticipated from the rerun procedures?
   e. What steps in the rerun can be skipped?
4. An out-of-balance condition that holds up critical path processing.
   a. What steps should the operator take to solve the problem?
   b. What are some likely causes?
   c. What are the risks if the shift director ignores the out-of-balance condition and continues with production?
   d. Is the magnitude of the out-of-balance condition important?
   e. Who should the shift director contact if unable to solve the problem? How much delay is acceptable before calling for help?

    f. If the decision is to ignore the message and continue, what should the users be told? Should they be asked to help in the problem analysis?

5. A key production support person cannot be reached.

    a. Who is the next in line to be called?

    b. How long should the shift director wait before calling the next individual?

    c. Should any management-level personnel be notified of the problem?

6. A sudden lack of material, such as paper or tapes.

    a. What are the names and phone numbers of the regular suppliers?

    b. Are there any local companies that provide materials on an emergency basis?

    c. What paperwork is necessary to purchase supplies on the weekends?

    d. Should the shift director make the decision or should the director call the manager?

7.3.2 Using the Special Procedures Manual

A special procedures book should be in a looseleaf binder with tabs so that the operations personnel can quickly locate the information they need. Staff members should periodically review the material—at least quarterly—to be aware that the information exists. It is not necessary to memorize the details, but simply to know that such facts are available and where to find them. The operations manager should verify in writing that all employees in the section who may be involved in special problem situations have actually reviewed the manual.

    Some installations put their special procedures book in an online text-editing or program development system. This eliminates the problems associated with paper, but it requires that operators and other staff members have access to at least one CRT at all times. If the online system is down or unavailable because of serious hardware problems, the special procedures documentation will be unavailable. For example, a shift supervisor might need to study the recovery procedures for a head crash on the same disk that supports the online text-editing system, but since the online application is down, the material itself is unavailable. The hardware problem could prevent employees from seeing the solution! Most installations that do store vital documentation on disk also print a hard-copy backup just for these rare but always possible situations.

Updating a special procedures book is just as important as updating run instructions. As the hardware, software, or applications environment changes, the special procedures book will need new sections to replace the sections deleted. It is important for the operations manager to critically examine the book and make changes when appropriate. Having too much useless information is as bad as not having enough useful facts—the net effect is the same.

7.4 AUTOMATED OPERATIONAL DOCUMENTATION

Creating and maintaining operational documentation such as run sheets, problem logs, and special procedures manuals is costly and time-consuming. Busy employees must be taken from other assignments and given enough resources to develop the initial documentation. Then operations and programming management must continually insist that each staff member keep the documents current. Obviously, this is expensive in terms of employee time, and data-processing experts have traditionally suggested the computer as a way to automate tasks that require large amounts of human effort. Some farsighted software companies have recognized this need and have developed automated packages that provide run sheets, flowcharts, and other operational documentation based on the job control language (or JCL, in IBM terminology). But automation is not always the answer to everything, as many systems analysts and frustrated users have discovered over the years. Can those packages actually help a data center? Or are they little more than expensive glitter?

The benefits of such a computerized system can be impressive, especially if the product uses the actual job control language and its run-time parameters to produce the documentation. A good software product will allow the operations department to choose documentation output that is very detailed or very summarized, depending on the particular need and circumstances. Eventually these products will allow the operations and programming staff to actually design the formats, in the same way that fourth-generation application development systems let users design their screens and hardcopy reports. A good product will allow online storage, maintenance, retrieval, and comprehensive search facilities.

Automated systems can have disadvantages, primarily when the operations staff cannot effectively use the documentation formats without major changes. Although it is always possible to force computer operators to accept what is available, such a practice lowers morale and creates resentment. If management decides to impose a specific form or system on the operations staff members without allowing them to participate in the design and testing phases, the operators may respond by simply ignoring the documentation. The advantage of having a form for run sheets, problem logs, and associated documentation designed in-house is that the staff members can help mold the output into a form most useful for them and their environment.

Although a purchased package can be a major breakthrough for a shop that has limited or virtually nonexistent documentation, operations managers should carefully compare the benefits of a purchased package to the advantages of a system designed specifically for their hardware, software, and applications. A ready-made product is easy to install, can produce documentation quickly, and usually takes less clerical effort to maintain. The in-house-designed forms (which can also be made into an automated system) have a format designed for an individual data center, but they do require more work from the operators and programmers in setting up the initial documentation. Fortunately, some vendors provide a free trial period to evaluate their automated system, which makes the comparison project relatively straightforward. As these systems become more sophisticated and flexible, they will become more and more attractive. But until these products do possess this flexibility, MIS managers must take a close look at the benefits of a purchased package compared to the inherent advantages of an in-house-designed system. The choice may be difficult.

7.5 MASTER SYSTEM DOCUMENTATION

Run sheets and assorted documentation are easier to use when organized into manuals (either hard-copy or represented by a file on disk) related to each application, or to each "logical unit" of operation. Most business data-processing installations use a specific application system as the unit of work, such as general ledger, inventory control, and accounts payable. These application-specific manuals allow immediate access to information when a question or problem appears.

But run sheets themselves do not describe an application in terms that allow operators and programmers to understand the flow of data among specific jobs, or among different production schedules. In a typical batch environment, daily jobs produce data that are fed into other daily, weekly, or monthly jobs. Problems and misunderstandings develop because the staff does not properly understand this data flow or system integration. Indeed, those employees in a data center rated as most knowledgeable may be those who have mastered this data flow concept! Therefore, another document called the "system flow" should be the first entry in the master system manual, and it should be designed for operators rather than programmers. Although the programming personnel obviously need similar information, their style and level of detail will probably be much different. Of course, any document that describes the operational data flow will still be helpful to new programmers or those employees who wish to learn the basics of the technical side of an unfamiliar application system.

Analysts traditionally use the standard flowchart to describe a computer system. This format works reasonably well if the writer puts considerable thought into selecting the appropriate level of detail. *A common mistake that renders many beautiful flowcharts useless is inclusion of too much detail.* Like run sheets, the guideline for a system flow diagram should be: What does the operator need to know?

The answers are never obvious. With too little information, the document will be unsatisfactory, and too much detail will obscure the important facts. The simplest approach is to have the operations staff members make detailed suggestions based on their own experience. Simply questioning a new operator who is trying to learn the systems is an excellent way to get feedback. Only by involving the operational staff members—who are the end users of this documentation—can the writer or manager select the optimum level of detail needed by the employees.

7.6 DATA CENTER STATISTICS REPORT

Business analysts look at the typical data center or operations department as an information factory, and therefore they suggest measuring the input and output of the computer room as one measures the performance of a manufacturing plant. Performance statistics are a concise, easily understood way of comparing the activities of the data center from one period to another. Without such measures, it becomes impossible to answer the question: How is the data center doing?

The answer is to publish a weekly and monthly statistics report that captures the most relevant data available. This allows MIS management, data center management, and everyone else in the division to understand the workload, problems, and production aspects of their data center. Figure 7.3 is a sample data center statistics report that can be modified to fit most environments. This report should be issued weekly, and for a monthly cycle it should be accompanied by a one- or two-page narrative that mentions the high points of the month. Statistics and raw numbers are important, but the narrative explanation will put those measures in the proper perspective.

7.7 SUMMARY OF KEY POINTS

☐ Run sheets should contain only the facts needed by the people who actually use them, such as computer operators

PRODUCTION	CURRENT WEEK	LAST WEEK	MONTH TO DATE	PREV. MONTH TO DATE	TY YEAR TO DATE	LY YEAR TO DATE
Jobs complete on time						
Jobs restarted						
Lost time for restarts						
Reruns						
Nights critical path complete by 0600						
Nights critical path late						
% critical path on time						
Total interrupts						
Hardware						
Application						
Software						
Unknown						

Others										
User response time										
0800										
1030										
1200										
1400										
1600										
1800										
Avg. batch turnaround										
Employee hours										
Worked										
Illness										
Overtime										
Training										
No. of employees										

Figure 7.3 Data Center Statistics Report

and tape librarians. They should not have information for nonusers, such as programmers and data analysts.

☐ One group or individual must have primary management control over run sheets and monitor the updating and distribution process. If no one is responsible for run sheets, no one will maintain them.

☐ Run sheets should answer the questions everyone knows will arise, but is afraid to ask. For example, when this job fails at 2:00 AM for this specific reason, what should the operator do? What are the effects if the problem cannot be resolved by 3:00 AM?

☐ Every significant problem in a data center should be tracked through a problem-reporting log that is easy to fill out and use.

☐ It is difficult to separate significant from nonsignificant problems. Expect mistakes. Provide realistic examples as guidelines.

☐ Run sheets alone are not adequate for handling every situation that will arise in a data center. A special procedures manual should contain information that tells how to manage actual and potential problems. This manual can also be a "disaster manual," although it describes other situations than disasters, such as taking a once-a-year physical inventory that dramatically affects the data center.

☐ Automated operation documentation can help, especially for shops that have virtually no existing documentation.

☐ Run sheets and other documentation should be organized into a master system book for each application or logical unit of processing.

☐ The data center statistics report is a simple but effective way to communicate some of the important measures of data performance.

☐ The monthly statistics report should include a description of the important facts that affected the results; raw numbers (even when they show trends) need some explanation.

chapter 8

Software Acquisition Documents

INTRODUCTION

Buying ready-made software is a common practice. Most companies purchase their bread-and-butter applications, such as payroll and general ledger, and some organizations buy virtually all their business systems from software vendors. Choosing the best package is difficult. The success or failure of any selection process depends partially on the quality of the written communication that flows between the vendor and MIS. This chapter has four carefully designed documents that will fit into almost any software methodology: a vendor evaluation survey, a sample letter of reference, a user questionnaire, and a software comparison chart. Anyone concerned with software acquisition can use these sample forms and associated procedures to make a better final selection. Systems analysts, technical writers, users, user department managers, and MIS executives can use these forms with only slight modifications.

The term "acquisition" immediately conjures up visions of legal contracts and purchasing agreements, but there is a lot more to the long, often frustrating software acquisition process than writing or revising a contract. Everything involved in acquisition is complicated, but the procedure has a greater chance for success if the team performing the package selection uses carefully engineered written communication. Good technical writing helps prevent problems and reduces the risk inherent in purchasing a software package. Conversely, inadequate written communication can lead to poor MIS and user decisions.

Software contracts *are* complicated and do require legal expertise. One needs only to survey the trade journals to see the multitude of companies suing vendors over packages and systems that did not perform according to expectations! In most situations, *the problems did not originate with the contract, but with the software acquisition process itself.* The selection group made a mistake, and the best contract in the world will not rectify that original error. For every business that sends its lawyers to the courtroom, there are fifty others that were equally disappointed by a software package but decided not to go through the long, involved drama of a lawsuit. Simply buying a package is easy, but selecting the "best" one is a complicated project.

Even the best lawyer cannot save a company from the ongoing pains of a poor software selection. The organization may survive, but the staff will pay a heavy price in terms of user dissatisfaction and MIS frustration. Effective technical communication during the selection and negotiation phase will help prevent incorrect selections.

Like system design documents, internal and external vendor-related materials should be part of a well-thought-out *software acquisition methodology.* Too often, however, MIS staffers are given only theoretical approaches and not sample formats they can modify for immediate use. This chapter provides documents that will fit into most software acquisition methodologies. For companies that do not have a formalized approach, these samples will help develop a rational and logical method of selecting software.

8.1 VENDOR EVALUATION FORMS

Once the project team members have selected the final packages for consideration (or even during the initial screening), they need detailed information about the vendor. When a company purchases a software package, it is also buying the people and organization behind the system. The larger the package, the more important the vendor's capabilities. When selecting a $400 microcomputer application, MIS will generally be satisfied if the system works! But when selecting a $400,000 manufacturing system that takes months to install, MIS will be vitally concerned with the vendor's ability to support the investment. Large, expensive, and complex applications require large, expensive, and complex installation efforts—the vendor may be a key to success or failure.

Figure 8.1 is a vendor questionnaire that will provide basic information about the company behind the product. This form can also gather information about organizations that are being considered for service contracts or consulting awards. In terms of software acquisition, this document has enough information for the team to judge the vendor's:

- Financial base
- Experience level
- Staff qualifications
- Ability to respond

Whereas these answers are necessary during the final evaluation stage, such *written* responses also furnish additional legal protection, because documents have some binding authority. Unfortunately, the degree of legal impact varies with the situation. In some cases, the documents have no legal standing. Nevertheless, experienced systems

Instructions to vendor: Please complete this survey form and return to the address listed on the cover letter within three weeks. Please attach any material requested and any other documents that you feel support your qualifications. Thank you.

Your name: _____ Title: _____

A.   *FINANCIAL BASE*

1. How long has your company been in business?

_____

2. Has ownership changed during the past five years? Yes ____ No ____ If yes, explain the timing and circumstances.

_____

_____

_____

_____

3. Are the current owners contemplating selling the business? Yes ____ No ____

4. How many employees do you have now? _____

How many do you plan to have in one year? _____

5. How many employees have you hired during the past twelve months? _____

6. How many employees have you lost during the past twelve months? _____

7. How long has the CEO been with the firm? _____

Figure 8.1 Vendor Evaluation Survey

8. Are you being sued? Yes ____ No ____ If yes, list each action and describe in an attachment.

9. Are you suing any other company? Yes ____ No ____ If yes, describe in a separate attachment.

10. Are you a public company? Yes ____ No ____ If yes, enclose last year's annual report.

11. List your gross sales for the past five years:

YEAR   **GROSS SALES**

_____   _____

_____   _____

_____   _____

_____   _____

_____   _____

12. In what year was your first software sale? _____

13. What is the total value of all software sales made since your company began? _____

14. What is the sales forecast for the next fiscal year? _____

15. List five trade publications in which you have advertised:

_____

_____

_____

_____

_____

Figure 8.1 (*Continued*)

16. List the name, address, and phone number of your bank.

_____

_____

_____

17. What is your Dun and Bradstreet number?

_____

B.   *THE PACKAGE*

1. When did you first sell this product? _____
2. Did you develop it yourself or did you purchase it from another company?

_____

_____

3. When was this product first developed? _____
4. How many major releases have you provided since it was first sold to customers? _____
5. How many installations do you have of this product?

_____

6. How many employees serve on "product enhancement" or development teams specifically for this product? _____
7. When is your next planned major release? _____
8. What are the next planned enhancements?

_____

_____

_____

Figure 8.1 Vendor Evaluation Survey *(Continued)*

9. Who represents you (e.g., your own people, independent sales organizations, or consultants)?

_____

_____

10. Do you have a 24-hour hotline?
Yes _____ No _____ If yes, what type of people handle phone calls?

_____

11. Is there an extra charge for hotline support? Yes _____ No _____

_____

12. Who backs up the hotline staff?

_____

13. What types of questions will the hotline staff _not_ answer?

_____

_____

_____

14. List the five best things about your system.

_____

_____

_____

_____

_____

Figure 8.1 (_Continued_)

15. List five weak points reported by customers.

_____

_____

_____

_____

_____

16. Will   you   provide   a   complete   client   list?
Yes _____ No _____ If yes, please attach.

17. List five reference sites we can contact. We will need names, addresses, and phone numbers.

_____

_____

_____

_____

_____

_____

_____

18. To your knowledge, has anyone purchased your package but failed to install it? If so, please describe the situation.

_____

_____

_____

_____

Figure 8.1   Vendor Evaluation Survey *(Continued)*

C.   *SERVICES*

1. Do you have multiple-site leasing agreements? _____

2. Do you provide consulting services? _____

At what rate? _____

For what purposes? _____

_____

_____

_____

_____

What is the background of your consultants?

_____

_____

During the last calendar year, about how much revenue did you derive from paid consulting services? _____
   List two companies that have purchased your consulting services during the past two years. Please provide the name, address, and phone number of someone we can contact for each company.

_____

_____

_____

_____

_____

_____

Figure 8.1   *(Continued)*

3. Do you have a user group?   Yes _____ No_____
During the last calendar year, how many times did the user group meet? _____
Does the user group control all or part of your development effort? If so, please explain. _____

_____

_____

_____

_____

_____

When did the user group form? _____

Who can we contact in the user group? _____

_____

_____

_____

4. When customers discover problems, who do they first contact? _____
For source code changes or fixes, do you give customers line number fixes or do you send a complete new module? _____
Besides major releases, do you have any revisions? _____
If yes, how often do they occur? _____

D.   *MANUFACTURING EXPERTISE*

1. How many APICS-certified employees do you have? _____
2. How many others are enrolled in the certification program? _____

Figure 8.1   Vendor Evaluation Survey *(Continued)*

3. In what positions are the certified employees?

_____

_____

_____

_____

4. How many Class A users do you have? _____
5. How many users do you have in the process industry? _____
6. How many of your users have purchased your other packages? _____
7. What is the average time required to fully implement your MRP? _____
8. What is the longest time taken to install your MRP? (Ignore companies that stop and start the implementation project.) _____
9. Do you provide guidelines (such as suggested task lists) for implementation? _____
10. Has your inventory control module ever interfaced directly with an automated storage/automated retrieval system? Yes _____ No _____ If yes, please describe.

_____

_____

_____

_____

11. What auditing firms have inspected and/or approved your suggested physical inventory accounting procedures? _____

_____

_____

_____

Figure 8.1 (_Continued_)

analysts and managers have learned that salespersons who tend to exaggerate slightly when chatting over coffee will lose that tendency when they must put their answers in writing.

Before using this questionnaire, the project team should eliminate those questions that do not apply to the system under consideration and add statements that reflect on the specific application. Section D of Figure 8.1 concerns a manufacturing environment and was designed for a project team considering an MRP-II (manufacturing resource planning) package. By replacing Section D, one can adapt the form for other business or scientific systems. These sections do not replace the detailed requirements, but rather summarize them in a format that can be easily understood. If this section is expanded, it will eventually become a "request for proposal" or RFP. But for a vendor evaluation survey or initial screening procedure, only the important requirements are listed. The purpose of a vendor evaluation survey is to narrow the field as quickly as possible.

8.2 LETTER OF REFERENCE

After the final candidates have been selected, the project team often calls or writes existing customers of each vendor. Analysts disagree as to the choice of a phone call or a letter. Which one gives the most useful information? Or should the systems analyst use both? A phone call has the advantage of being easier for both the analyst and the customer and can often elicit opinions that many people will refuse to put down on paper! On the minus side, however, even the best-prepared phone call cannot provide answers to every detailed question. Furthermore, verbal discussions are transitory, and unless the listener is tape recording the conversation, it is seldom possible to remember all the information given.

The best approach is to use both. A phone call can be used to contact the person, and this contact can be followed up with a carefully designed letter and questionnaire.

Letters and survey documents require planning and effort, but they are more permanent than a phone call. Unfortunately, such letters also have a frustrating habit of being ignored. Some companies that send out ten letters of reference will feel fortunate if three are returned. This "throw it in the wastebasket" attitude is not simply random; rather, it is predictable. For example, the spirit of cooperation rises with the cost and complexity of the package. A manager responsible for a $5,000 utility may be less likely to respond than one who uses a $400,000 manufacturing package. Companies with complex purchased applications are often very willing to furnish information to other organizations if their comments will not get them into legal difficulties. Their motivation may come from a desire to help fellow professionals, or to establish friendly contact with other companies, or simply to get back at the vendor for doing a poor job. *The phone call should be an attempt to uncover that motivation.*

Having a company respond to a questionnaire is encouraging, but the actual value of the information depends in part on the respondent's personal attitudes.

The accompanying questionnaire should be brief—most ten-page questionnaires automatically wind up in the wastebasket. Busy MIS professionals and users often refuse to spend their valuable time completing long, involved documents that will never help them directly. A one-page questionnaire is ideal, although two pages are usually acceptable. Anything over three pages may disappear forever!

It is not easy to determine the *best* person in an organization to contact. Sales representatives may provide the name of the person they are most familiar with or of someone who is unlikely to criticize their product. In the same company, however, *one may find differing opinions on the same product.* The director of manufacturing may not be satisfied with an MRP system because it does not provide adequate production reports, whereas the purchasing manager may think the system is the greatest invention since fast-food hamburgers. The software analyst may hate a disk space utility software package at the same time the operations manager extolls the virtues of the system that saves one hour of overnight processing. Letters of reference and survey questionnaires are valuable, but they should not always be taken literally—everyone who relies on such documents must understand their limitations. *The opinions expressed in questionnaires are a function of the individual's personal experiences, job responsibilities, and familiarity with the package as well as the amount of sleep the individual got last night.*

The way to get around that potential problem is simple: Send the material to at least *two* people in the same organization, preferably in different departments. Although there is nothing to prevent those two or more people from collaborating, the project team still has a better chance of getting a valid opinion. If responses from those individuals differ greatly, the analysts may wish to recontact them by phone for further details.

Figure 8.2 is a reference letter to a person previously contacted by phone, and Figure 8.3 is the corresponding questionnaire. Every survey document should be designed for both the specific application and the type of respondent. Some analysts create what they consider an all-purpose form that can be answered by several groups of people. This is a mistake! The respondents are doing the project team a favor and should not be forced to search over extraneous information. If the team needs answers from the viewpoints of MIS, payroll, accounting, and internal auditing, it should provide a custom-designed questionnaire for the contact in each area. The payroll manager does not want to be bothered reading questions on data base access efficiency meant for the software expert.

8.3 SOFTWARE COMPARISON CHARTS

Once all the information has been compiled from letters of reference, requirements documents, RFPs, and detailed discussions, the project team summarizes the important points in *comparison documents*. These handy charts compare the

Ms. Gretta Grimy
Production Manager
Dirt Enterprises, Inc.
9046 Yucky Avenue
Muddy Flats, Iowa 40567

Dear Ms. Grimy:

Thanks for your offer to give us your opinions on the Worm Farm Management System you had developed by your parent corporation, Wonderful Widgets. As I mentioned, Wonderful Widgets has now turned WOFAMS into a package we at Consolidated Widgets may use for our own worm subsidiary. I don't have to tell you that it's hard telling which end is which in the worm business, and we need every bit of computerized help we can get.

Attached is a short questionnaire and self-addressed stamped envelope.

For your information, we have also sent a questionnaire to your controller, Terrance Tightwad III, for his evaluation of the financial reports.

Again, thanks very much for your help. We greatly appreciate your cooperation.

Sincerely,

Bernadette Brown
Senior Systems Analyst
Division of Worms

attach.

Figure 8.2 Letter of Reference

1. When did you first install WOFAMS? _____

2. How long did your installation take? _____

3. Did you have any unexpected problems with the installation process? _____

_____

_____

4. Please rate WOFAMS, with 5 the highest and 1 the lowest:

   General effectiveness 1 2 3 4 5
   System accuracy   1 2 3 4 5
   Ease of use   1 2 3 4 5
   Reliability   1 2 3 4 5
   Completeness   1 2 3 4 5

5. What is (are) the best thing(s) about WOFAMS?

_____

_____

_____

6. What did you like least about WOFAMS?

_____

_____

_____

7. Are you satisfied with the production reports?

   Daily _____

   Weekly _____

   Monthly _____

8. Are the data entry screens easy to use? _____

Figure 8.3 Sample Questionnaire for Evaluating a Package

9. Are you satisfied with the online edits? _____

10. Are the audit trails satisfactory to your production people? Yes _____ No _____ Do you have any suggestions for better auditing? _____

_____

11. Is your online response time acceptable? Is it always less than three seconds? _____

12. Did you work with Wonderful Widgets during the installation phase? _____

If yes, did they meet your needs? _____

_____

13. Have you worked with them since installation? _____

If yes, please comment on their service. _____

_____

14. How would you rate their user documentation?

_____

15. In general, on a scale of 1 (the lowest) to 5 (the highest), how would you rate WOFAMS as a generalized system to handle the Worm Farm Business? _____

Thank you very much for your comments.

Figure 8.3 (*Continued*)

packages according to the most important criteria, as determined by the team. The value of a comparison chart depends on the thought put into it. A good chart will allow the decision makers to visually scan the document and rate the possibilities in a logical manner. A poorly designed or executed chart, on the other hand, can waste weeks and months of effort by confusing an already complex situation. *The job of a software acquisition team is not only to gather all important information about the packages and vendors, but to present those facts, opinions, and judgments in an easy-to-understand way.*

System analysts and technical writers always have a serious responsibility to the companies that pay their salaries, but their responsibility is even more serious when performing software acquisition studies. By manipulating software comparison documents, an analyst can easily slight one vendor and give an unfair advantage to another. This is unethical at the very least (if not illegal) and violates the basis of professional responsibility. Because most senior managers and users would rather read summaries and comparison charts than detailed requirements, the ultimate choice may be affected by the *tone* of the chart or summary. *Every software acquisition and vendor contact document should be reviewed by at least one other professional to verify its objectivity.*

Although requirements are often developed through discussions, arguments, and eventual compromise, a good comparison document goes beyond those specific requirements and looks at a software acquisition from a company-wide perspective. That is, the document evaluates the software package on the basis of five important factors:

1. How does each package satisfy the A-B-C requirements for the user and MIS?
2. How does each vendor look in terms of probable support?
3. How does each software package fit in with other projects, activities, or purchases as listed in the long-range MIS plan?

4. What are the relative risks of each package and vendor?

5. What are the total external, internal, and ongoing costs of each system?

A document that specifies only user requirements is therefore presenting only one-fifth of the "software acquisition circle"—the other four-fifths may actually determine which system is best for the organization! Software purchases are business rather than purely technical decisions. User requirements are certainly important and should be given a prominent place in the comparison document, but other factors are equally important and must be included in the comparison. If the chart ignores vital business-oriented considerations, the senior decision makers may eventually ignore the comparison document. This is just as frustrating to the project team members as it is to the managers who appointed them, even if the analysts and technical writers have done an outstanding job analyzing user requirements. Their only mistake was to underestimate the scope of their responsibilities.

Are the five factors of requirements, vendor support, long-range "fit," risks, and costs always necessary? In any given situation, one or more of those considerations may not apply, or perhaps another one should be substituted. Selecting the factors that will determine the ultimate choice is not always simple. The technical writer should carefully poll the decision makers before creating the document to obtain their actual criteria for making final software decisions. If they reply with the obvious statement, "Why, on the basis of user requirements, of course," the technical writer should repeat the question. Either they did not understand the request, or they are being evasive, or they are not true decision makers. If the analyst team members fail to get cooperation, they must make their own guesses, but they must always go beyond user and MIS requirements in their summary documents.

For both user and MIS requirements, comparison charts can use either simple yes/no answers or a more sophisticated ratings matrix. There are at least two ways to quantify judgments. First, one can say that category A requirements are obviously more important than category B requirements. (This chapter assumes that the analyst team is using the classic A-B-C approach to requirements definition, as explained in Chapter 3). Therefore, the technical writer can assign a weight of 3 to all category A requirements, a weight of 2 to category B requirements, and a weight of 1 to category C requirements. These relative weights are purely arbitrary—one could assign category A a value of 6, category B a value of 3, and category C a value of 1. With the yes/no checks, if a package meets six category A requirements, it will receive a score of 18 (6 × 3) for category A. If it meets 12 category B requirements, it will receive a rating of 24 (12 × 2) for category B compliance. This method is better than merely counting the number of checkmarks in each category, because it provides numeric totals for comparison.

The second way to use a matrix, called the *double ratings* method, is to assign weights for each requirement *within* a category. For example, a specific payroll system (which involves transmission of confidential information) may provide "adequate" data security, which constitutes a category A entry in a requirements document. But another package may have sophisticated security procedures that should be rated as "outstanding." The yes/no method would evaluate the two systems equally (each would receive a score of 3 for data security). The analyst, however, needs a simple way to explain that one package is superior and to include this advantage in the total score.

By using a 1 to 3 scale *within* each category, a value of 3 can be assigned to the package that has superior data security features. Thus its score for data security becomes 18 (3 × 6). The 6 is the standard rating for all category A requirements, and the 3 is the value for this package, because it has exceptional data security features. Other packages that meet only the basic data security requirement would receive a standard 6 (6 × 1), because the default value would always be 1. The double ratings approach may provide more accurate totals for compari-

This chart was developed by the Software Acquisition Team of Consolidated Widgets for the purpose of selecting a comprehensive Worm Farm Management System. Our three finalists are WOFAMS (from Wonderful Widgets), SLIME (from Muddy Data Systems), and ICKY (from Underground Systems, Inc).

This chart compares our finalists in five areas:

1. User and MIS requirements (broken down by A-B-C priority)
2. Vendor support and performance
3. How each package fits into our long-range plan
4. Risks
5. Costs—direct, indirect, and ongoing

	WOFAMS	SLIME	ICKY
1. User and MIS requirements— inventory control			
Category A (required— base value = 6):			
Real time updating	1	1	0
Inquiry by length of worm	0	1	1
Physical inventory capability	3	2	1
Random locator system	1	2	0
Parent-child access	3	1	2
Group item numbers	1	1	1
Interface to purchasing system	2	0	0
MIS:			
Hierarchical data base	1	0	1
At least six CRTs online simultaneously	1	0	1

Figure 8.4 Software Acquisition Comparison Chart

	WOFAMS	SLIME	ICKY
Category B (suggested —base value = 3):			
Inquiry by color	1	1	1
Update by color group	1	1	0
Average costing by worm	2	1	0
MIS: automatic backout by tran code	1	0	1
MIS: inquiry by tran code	0	2	1
Category C (nice to have—base value = 1):			
Accidental death history file	2	0	2
Suggested replenishment by warehouse	3	2	2
MIS transaction history file	1	0	0
Total raw scores for inventory requirements	13	8	7
Scores with weights for A (6), B (3), and C(1)	99	69	55
2. Vendor support and performance			
In business more than 5 years	yes	no	no
In business more than 2 years	yes	no	yes
Number of employees	79	32	12
Dun and Bradstreet trend	up	down	up
Dun and Bradstreet general evaluation	good	risky	good
Hotline support	no	yes	no

Figure 8.4 Software Acquisition Comparison Chart *(Continued)*

	WOFAMS	SLIME	ICKY
Consulting support (chargeable)	yes	yes	no
Number of major releases	6	3	2
Client survey	good	fair	mixed
Annual sales (millions of dollars)	45	18	6
Next year's sales forecast (millions of dollars)	49	23	18
MIS comfort level with technical reps	good	good	poor

3. **Interfacing with our long-range MIS plan**

	WOFAMS	SLIME	ICKY
Supports at least two other data bases	yes	no	yes
Vendor has purchasing system available now	yes	no	no
Handles multiple worm farm locations	yes	yes	yes
Could use MIS information center	yes	no	no
Runs on minis (distributed option)	yes	no	yes
Vendor provides contract programming	no	yes	yes
Vendor has accounting systems ready	yes	no	no

4. **Risks**

	WOFAMS	SLIME	ICKY
Vendor going out of business (estimate)	nil	maybe	low
Package will be obsolete in three years	no	maybe	no

Figure 8.4 (*Continued*)

	WOFAMS	SLIME	ICKY
Could handle government regulations if worms become controlled substance	yes	yes	maybe
5. **Costs** (thousands of dollars)			
Purchase price	120	94	75
Interface to existing systems	59	40	65
Vendor maintenance per year	12	12	7
Internal installation cost	10	10	10
Total direct expense to vendor	120	94	75
Internal MIS expense	69	50	75
Total indirect and direct	189	144	150

Figure 8.4 Software Acquisition Comparison Chart *(Continued)*

sons and helps the entire project team by forcing the analysts and users to understand the relative value of each requirement.

Figure 8.4 illustrates a software acquisition comparison chart using the five basic considerations for selecting the "best fit" software package. The user and MIS requirements section uses a double ratings method. The total score in the requirements section explains the "relative fit" of the most important requirements. This matrix format takes a little more work, but the results are always worth the effort.

8.4 SUMMARY OF KEY POINTS

☐ When buying a software package, the organization also "buys" the vendor—its people, resources, and degree of support. Using the vendor questionnaire helps the team discover strengths and weaknesses.

☐ Before sending a letter of reference to gather opinions about a package or vendor, call the person being solicited and ask permission. Casually ask about his general attitude toward the package. Don't depend on the phone call, but use the verbal comments to supplement your understanding of the written responses.

☐ Send the reference letter to at least two people in the same organization—never depend on one response. Select people in different areas who use the package. Followup with a probing phone call if the responses differ greatly.

☐ After collecting all information about packages and their vendors, use a software comparison chart to present the findings. The chart must include nontechnical factors (such as cost) as well as user/MIS requirements. Reviewers need to see data on each candidate arrayed in a side-by-side format.

☐ The software comparison chart should be checked by people outside the project team to verify that it does not give unfair advantage to one vendor.

☐ The classic A-B-C requirements should be weighted so that category A requirements are worth more than category B requirements. The double ratings method uses weights within a category to further differentiate among packages.

chapter *9*

Programming and Technical Documentation

INTRODUCTION

MIS professionals complain—with valid reasons—about the sad state of their own technical documentation. Yearly internal and external audits repeatedly point to inadequate or out-of-date internal documentation. Even organizations that pride themselves on the quality of their user documentation may neglect documenting systems for their own employees. This chapter describes the purpose and business justification for documentation and emphasizes that internal documentation must follow predefined standards. Internal documentation has three overlapping purposes: to help with system maintenance, to aid in research or investigative work, and to prepare for eventual program replacement. The answer book and system log will provide a useful resting place for other important but often overlooked information. This chapter is for all technical employees, technical writers, and MIS managers.

Well-written and *useful* technical documents are so rare that they are often treated as works of art and shown proudly to visiting dignitaries. Even software companies that sell programs and complete systems as their primary business often admit that their own internal documentation is vastly inferior to their user documentation. The key term is "useful," for much of the documentation was never designed according to logical rules and procedures, but simply *exists*. Internal documentation that is not carefully planned is about as useless as a payroll system thrown together without precise rules. Both are more trouble than they are worth. Computer hardware and software have come a long way since the 1960s, but the complaints of those early programmers are still heard in the late 1980s. If documentation exists, it must help the MIS staff members in their day-to-day work assignments. If it fails that test, the documentation has little practical value.

Technical documentation deserves as much planning, thought, and preparation as design documents and user manuals. Many of the considerations that apply to such diverse documents as feasibility statements and requirements definitions should apply to program-level documentation. The principles of effective written communication are just as important when one programmer writes information for another technician.

9.1 THE PURPOSE OF TECHNICAL DOCUMENTATION

Before writing any internal documentation, one must define the *purpose* of documenting that particular program or module. The reason must justify the time and expense involved in creating the documentation. The obvious premise for providing internal documentation is that the original programmer and analyst team will not be supporting the program forever. Others will assume responsibility, and they will not have the same intimate familiarity with the program as the original team. Without such detailed knowledge of the program and system, the new supporting team will require larger and more expensive resources. However, this scenario is only one justification for internal documentation.

There are three basic reasons for documenting a computer program or unit of software:

1. To help with the inevitable maintenance effort by quickly imparting at least a generalized understanding of the module to other programmers or analysts

2. To efficiently explain the details of processing (or logic) to answer questions posed by users and other MIS employees

3. To list information about a program so that it can eventually be replaced

In any given situation, one or more of these reasons is likely to apply. Perhaps the staff realizes that the *purchase order generate* program will be subject to periodic maintenance requests. The internal documentation should therefore be pointed toward the specific needs of a maintenance programmer. Or the program logic may be very complex and the original programmer may foresee many requests from the users to clarify the options or costing logic. Such a complex program needs documentation that explains the processing in easy-to-understand terms so that the programmer is not forced to laboriously trace logic paths in the code. In other cases, a manager may know that a given program is slated for replacement and the programmer should be directed to list the program's details for use by future analyst teams as base requirements. This last justification truly demands a long-range management view.

Unless the programmer or manager who supervises the technical staff understands the specific justification (or justifications) of internal documentation, valuable time and resources may be wasted. Documentation styles, content, and format will differ for each of the three reasons given above. If, however, none of these reasons apply, the effort may not be justified. For example, if management is relatively certain that a particular program will not need maintenance or enhancements, the first reason is eliminated. If the processing logic is simple or thoroughly documented in a user manual, the second reason is not valid. And if that same piece of software will most likely never be replaced, *internally documenting that particular unit of software is not justified.* Obviously, this example is extreme, but the principle is valid: a programmer should never start documenting until there is a clear reason for the documentation. Understanding the purpose will help the writer make the documentation meaningful.

Defining the purpose helps the programmer systematically analyze the audience. As with a system design proposal or user manual, every piece of technical documentation is written for specific groups of people with specific needs. When the purpose of documenting a program is to help with future maintenance problems, the programmer understands that the documentation is being written for other programmers working in a maintenance rather than a development environment. The audience (usually only one programmer or analyst) will need information that helps to analyze the program and make changes safely. If the original programmer mentally assumes the position of a maintenance programmer, the documentation can be directed toward the unique and sometimes high-pressure needs of maintenance.

9.2 STANDARDS FOR TECHNICAL DOCUMENTATION

Standards for internal documentation are not simply nice to have; they are a basic necessity. Technical documentation is seldom read casually; rather, it is typically used in time-critical situations. Programmers must quickly understand how a module works, and they should not have to spend valuable company time adapting to a new style of internal documentation in order to understand the program. When programs are internally documented in varying styles, a significant relearning period is required every time a programmer moves to a different module, and the *frustration factor* increases with every change. Each program or module written in a specific language should use the same format for its internal documentation. A programmer who has gone through one module will find the next one slightly easier *if the internal comments and documentation follow the same general format.* If the modules have differing styles, each attempt to understand another module will be more difficult. Only through consistently applied standards can all programmers, analysts, and managers realize the potential advantages of internal documentation.

9.3 JUSTIFYING INTERNAL DOCUMENTATION

Before internal documentation can become a practical departmental policy, management must evaluate the true economic value of good documentation for programs and modules. MIS management should apply the same type of cost and benefits analysis that they apply to user projects. The financial exercise of justifying documentation is very healthy, and one should never accept documentation merely because the "experts" say it is needed. For example, why should MIS spend a week of additional programmer time on a project that is already finished just to develop internal documentation? If the users are satisfied, is it worthwhile spending forty hours on documentation when there are always high-priority projects waiting in the wings? In the long-range view, does it make good business sense?

If the rationale falls into one of the three previously mentioned categories, the answer is a definite yes, especially in regard to routine production support. Maintenance consumes a large portion of many MIS budgets, and one reason for this unfortunate situation is that programmers assigned to application systems have a difficult time understanding the source code. This is not a result of incompetence, poor training, or lack of effort, but rather the fact that most application systems are written in third-generation languages such as COBOL and are difficult to understand. Internal documentation—when properly done—helps remove the mystery and speeds up the maintenance effort.

Whereas it is difficult to immediately provide quantitative justification, senior MIS management should have enough personal experience with production support requirements to understand the validity of that argument. Internal documentation is a good investment when *analyzed via the MIS long-range plan, because it reduces the maintenance effort.* If, however, management takes only a more narrow, short-term view, internal documentation is a losing investment. If MIS managers are truly to develop business skills, they must stop looking at their departments with a day-to-day orientation and discover the long-range business view. Internal documentation is nothing more or less than another business investment.

9.4 THE DATA DICTIONARY

The heart of any business application system is the collection of data elements used to reflect both permanent and *temporary* information (i.e., fields that are calculated or serve as "work variables"). A data dictionary describes these data elements in the following terms:

- Name
- Identification number
- Range values
- Internal structure (i.e., the format used in the computer)
- External format (i.e., the format or formats available for display)
- Editing characteristics
- Allowed alternate names
- Description

An application system written without a data dictionary may have different names for the same field, or the same name may refer to different data elements. The size of a data element passed from program to program or file to file may vary. Perhaps each programmer invented fields that were thought to be meaningful but that are actually confusing to users or other programmers. Although data base management systems help solve such problems by enforcing a common file or data structure for permanent data fields, only a comprehensive data dictionary will give true control over the company's entire information base.

The advantages of a data dictionary are as follows:

- Each program uses the same data element names, which prevents confusion.
- Programmers need less time to develop programs, since data have been predefined.
- Data have the same characteristics throughout the application system or systems.
- Users and technicians share a common definition of each data element.
- Library scans can pinpoint all occurrences of a specific data element, which helps in both maintenance and development projects.

Although simple in concept, implementing a data dictionary for existing application systems involves a major commitment of time and resources. Should management require a retrofit of all production systems to use the data dictionary? The answer depends on the degree of disorder. If the original programmers attempted to use some degree of consistency for names and definitions, the project may be costly but feasible. If, however, the developers followed their own whims, the project will be virtually impossible. But even if technically feasible, senior management will seriously question the payback of a retrofit. In many cases, a data dictionary should be used only with new applications.

An *active* dictionary is one that is an integral part of a system development procedure—the programmers must use the dictionary to create programs and data structures. A *passive* dictionary is a voluntary reference tool, and its value depends on how well the developers adhere to it. An active dictionary is the better choice.

9.5 DOCUMENTING PROGRAMS FOR MAINTENANCE PURPOSES

In COBOL programs, the identification division is the obvious starting point for easy-to-find documentation, but other languages do not have such formalized locations. However, programs written in PL/I, BASIC, and ASSEMBLER can easily provide a similar information, and in the same general sequence as COBOL.

Every program needs two titles: a *technical* name that describes the module from the traditional MIS programming viewpoint and an *application* title related to the program's business purpose. This second title (often used as a subtitle) should be meaningful to a user or systems analyst. It is difficult to develop a single title that is meaningful to everyone. Usually both titles will convey enough information for the two groups that typically inquire about programs. Titles, incidentally, are not cast in stone. *As programs evolve (usually to encompass more functions), their titles should be changed to match their new orientation.* Changing a program name that has existed for ten years does cause confusion at first, but the situation is even worse for programmers facing a new program with an incorrect or inappropriate title.

MIS textbooks insist that all programs include the name of the author and the date they were written, but such facts are only marginally important. In a typical maintenance environment, few people care when a program was written, and even fewer know or care to know the name of the original author. Once programmers have completed a module and turned it over to another person or group, they are generally free of any responsibility.

The purpose of a program is often partially explained by the titles, but the programmer should write several sentences fully describing the *purpose* of the module as it relates to input and output. For example, the purpose of program PO9000 may be to accept purchase order transactions from the user, apply them against the item and vendor data base, create written purchase orders, and generate open order transactions. This statement not only summarizes the logic, but gives the reader a basic understanding of *why* the program is important and what it does. When programmers do not grasp the purpose behind a program, they are missing the essential ingredient that will allow them to understand how the program fits into the application system. Without that basic understanding, maintenance is even more difficult and frustrating. Comprehending a program is like learning brain surgery: the student does not simply pick up a scalpel and start slicing away before knowing why the brain is an important organ. The macro-to-micro or general-to-specific approach is still best.

The programmer also should describe the *inputs* in another paragraph. Most computer programs have inputs from users, transaction files, or master files. When documentation does exist in the typical MIS department, it usually contains information about data, but existing file documentation tends to be confusing. Too often a programmer will simply list the seven files into a module, when actual file names are meaningful only to technical people who already understand the program. Instead, input should be described both in technical terms, such as by specific file names, and in terms of types of information. A purchase order file can be called MPO9170 and can also be described *in data terms* as a transaction file having item-level and header PO triggers. Both descriptions are correct, but they convey different meanings. It is relatively simple to judge the completeness of a paragraph describing input. If a sophisticated user cannot understand the data flow portion of the internal documentation, the comments in the program are not satisfactory.

The *processing* should be described in overview terms even if it duplicates some of the information provided in the purpose section. Important transactions should be mentioned (it is usually impractical to list all the transactions in a program), along with their effects on the output. For maintenance purposes, the programmer should give only a brief summary of the processing logic, since many standard maintenance requests deal with input and output rather than detailed logic changes.

The *output* should be documented in the same manner as the input, with each output described in *two* ways. For example, the programmer could describe the PORPG file in technical terms as a report file that is passed to a multilevel sort utility, and then describe the same file in application terms as a file having purchase order header, item-level, and

summary report records. Users in the purchasing department may not relate to "multilevel sort utilities," but they
can understand purchase order header and line-item
records. Programmers writing documentation must think
like technical people one moment and users the next. By
providing internal documentation that focuses on these differing mind-sets, the original programmer will be doing the
department a valuable service.

9.6 DOCUMENTING PROGRAMS TO EXPLAIN LOGIC

Many application systems (especially complex business or
scientific packages) require programmers to "explain" the
internal logic or trace specific conditions within a program.
Maintenance and production support in many installations
has been jokingly referred to as the "tell me why" function!
The only way to avoid this time-consuming and frustrating
task is to have specialized documentation in the logic sections that is usually updated as programmers discover new
information about a module.

For example, a request that arises frequently with many
purchasing systems is for an explanation of a calculated
item cost when the vendor provides various levels of discounts, such as quantity and price breakpoints. The purchase order is often hard to understand when multiple factors affect the final item cost. Although the original system
design document may have specified the "planned" logic,
the programmer may have misunderstood or found additional combinations not covered in the original document.
Even when the system design was virtually complete,
applications grow of their own volition as the business environment becomes more complex. Program logic often
becomes more involved every year. Each program or
module in such applications should have internal comments
labeled "processing," and as new facts are discovered, the
programmer should faithfully add them to the module. The
concern of programmers should be for the long-range
benefit of their professional associates. For example, if the
programmer discovers that the module gives precedence to

the weight breakpoint over the quantity discount, that piece of information should be preserved through internal comments in the logic section. *Every investigation that takes more than thirty minutes of actual programmer or analyst time should be documented.*

Even in the best-managed installation with a consistent program of updating user documentation, the results of such investigations are not always reflected in the user manuals. Therefore, the programming and technical staff members must preserve their own investment in resources by capturing the results of their many research assignments permanently in the source code. If documented neatly, such comments will not clutter up a program. Six months or a year later, when another user asks the same question, the information will be readily available in the program. The programmer will still have to find the correct module, but it will not be necessary to take a day, a week, or a month to trace the code and determine the priority of price discounts. The next user will be happier than the first, who had to wait a day, a week, or a month. The programming manager will be happier because it will not be necessary to expend significant resources to answer "Another darn fool question that must have been asked ten times during the past five years." By simply talking with programmers, MIS management can estimate the time savings with this type of internal documentation. Answering questions that have been answered before is both frustrating and unproductive.

Internal logic documentation should explain the *options* available in a program. User options are often the hardest to understand. When new options are added to a system, the user documentation may fail to list them or may not specify all their effects. The option itself may be simple, but the ultimate results can be confusing! Putting such information in the source code itself is often the only way that MIS can preserve it.

9.7 FLOWCHARTS

Flowcharts are controversial. Some MIS professionals feel that flowcharts are *obviously* required to understand a program, module, system, or entire business application. Others approve of flowcharts in theory but in practice find them either too detailed or not detailed enough, or either too simple or too complicated to decipher. The same programmer or analyst may think they are wonderful one day and a waste of time the next! Their actual value lies somewhere in between. Flowcharts can be valuable when *the originator understands the purpose of each flowchart and writes for the appropriate audience.* Like internal documentation, flowcharts should come in two varieties: one for the technical expert and another for those who wish to understand data flow or general business function. Flowcharts as a tool are not intrinsically useful or useless; it is their suitability for a specific purpose that determines their ultimate value. It is difficult to create a single flowchart that can be understood by more than one type of person, except for a very high-level overview.

Traditionally, programmers and systems analysts have used their trusty template and sharp pencil to produce flowcharts. For obvious reasons, the eraser was often used almost as much as the pencil. At a slightly more sophisticated level, programmers used different colors to emphasize relationships and groupings. But flowcharting has long been a mechanical, time-consuming, and often tedious job. Developing the information necessary to create a flowchart may be challenging, but the laborious process of slowly drawing a square, rectangle, or circle has caused many programmers and analysts to take shortcuts. Some have postponed drawing flowcharts until the manager or supervisor has forgotten about the documentation assignment. Others have conveniently forgotten some details that should have been left in.

Even more difficult than creating the original flowchart is making *changes* to an existing handwritten chart! What programmer wants to redraw an entire page of symbols merely to insert a newly added file or logic option? Even when accurate flowcharts were created when the program was put in production, they are seldom maintained. Therefore, many programmers routinely avoid using existing flowcharts, because they are usually inaccurate. They would rather laboriously work through the code themselves. Flowcharts may be useful, but mechanical difficulties make them hard to work with.

The solution is an automated online graphics package that uses standard EDP flowcharting symbols. The system should provide basic word-processing printing facilities, such as printing specific pages, rearranging blocks, copying symbols, and global editing. Text and graphics must be on the same page (and CRT screen). Such packages are a virtual necessity in today's MIS organization.

But relatively few MIS departments have seriously considered automated flowcharting systems for documenting existing systems. This reluctance to purchase a documentation package is unfortunate, since other professions have consistently forged ahead of MIS in terms of using computers to aid their own productivity. Accountants quickly discovered the simple but powerful spreadsheet on a low-cost microcomputer, and engineers pushed their companies to utilize computer-assisted design (CAD) systems. In each case, the justification was simply better use of a professional's time and a corresponding increase in productivity. Programmers do not absolutely need automated flowcharting packages (at least for documenting existing systems), any more than accountants absolutely need computerized spreadsheets, but the improvement in productivity will be just as great. Eventually MIS managers will realize that computer technology should also help the professionals in their own departments.

9.8 THE ANSWER BOOK

Every system, subsystem, or logical group of programs needs a document that answers routine questions about that unit. Many problems or potential difficulties with a system are not related to actual program errors or mistakes. Rather, they pertain to the operational environment and are impossible to document in specific programs; nor are they appropriate for inclusion in system manuals. Information on these problems is classified as "miscellaneous" information that a few key individuals keep in their heads but very important to maintenance programmers and analysts. This *answer book* is a real lifesaver in solving production support problems. Typical questions covered in an answer book might be:

- Why does that system take so long to execute?
- Can the run time ever be reduced? If so, how?
- When you rerun this application, what are the implications? What are the possible side-effects?
- What research techniques are best to use when resolving a production problem?
- Who in the user community can or should approve program changes?
- Does this system have any legal implications for the company?
- Why do these programs give us so many problems?
- Who is the current MIS expert on these modules?
- What are some good suggestions for testing program changes?
- Are standard JCL test decks available?
- Are there any good ideas for improving the performance of this unit that have not been logged in the pending project file?

The answer book should be a relatively informal document written strictly for the technical staff. Every time an answer is developed as part of normal production support, the originator can simply add the question and corresponding answer to the book. Of course, a word processor or online text editor is always best, but the information must be accessible to any authorized member of the programming or systems staff at any time. A manual locked in a manager's office is worthless at 2:00 AM! Miscellaneous information has solved many a crisis in the busy world of MIS.

9.9 THE SYSTEM LOG

Application systems are like living organisms—they constantly evolve through maintenance, enhancements, and modifications required by other projects. Users constantly demand improvements and changes, and MIS personnel modify applications for their own benefit. Such changes to a system are the leading cause of production problems, user dissatisfaction, and unresolved questions, all of which consume large portions of valuable MIS resources. The actual change may work, but its impact may not be felt until the next weekly, monthly, or yearly processing cycle. Some mistakes may be caught years after the program or system has been modified or rerun. The situation becomes more complicated when no one in MIS or the user community remembers exactly what happened. When did that particular change take place, and what was the purpose? When was the system last rerun, and what steps were skipped because they were "not needed"? Human memory is fallible, and the staff may have turned over several times since the rerun last year. Only the written word survives.

The alternative is to maintain a *system log* for every application system or subsystem. The purpose of this document is to track MIS history, because *history will often provide the answers or at least a clue to the probable answer!* Simply having a time log of each major event related to a system's life cycle is also helpful for planning and audit purposes.

A typical system log might be:

04/09/85 Put in production by J. Kenney and W. Williams. Had to restore the I104 data base twice because of errors in update program PO50BA (skipped each receipt transaction).

05/03/85 Corrected errors in handling transaction code 04 and 05 (item level PO triggers), which were dropping off the last item in every PO. PO numbers 34000–34987 have been affected and will not clear out for at least four months.

05/18/85 Bad tape on PO675 input caused abend, and we recreated all PO transactions. Had difficulty with warehouses 5, 6, and 8. Impossible to verify that every PO trigger was recreated. Expect nasty calls for several weeks. Users must audit report 560 and put in manual POs if we missed their data during recreate.

06/23/85 Implemented Phase II project, which corrected seven major errors in PO445 and PO446. See Phase II project description (S. Bernard) for details.

06/24/85 Phase II caused errors—POs from three warehouses were on each other's reports. Implemented fix (see fix log 85-129 in Operations for details). Had to backout data base updates for night of 06/23/85, and restored data base I1055 and I0195 to 06/23/85. Reran jobs 14, 15, and 16, but skipped 17.

The style is simple and direct, because people who read system logs need only the basic facts. They simply want to know what happened, in what sequence, and where to go for additional detail. The value of a system log depends on management's absolute insistence that it be kept up to date and accessible to all authorized persons. The drawback with any system log is determining *which* events should be included. If some technical people incorporate every one-line fix and there are many changes or problems with a given application, the log may become massive. If that happens, one individual must assume control and insist that only "major events" be logged. Obviously, it is impossible to always predict which event has the potential of becoming a serious problem in the future, but someone must make the initial decision. After six months to a year, management can reevaluate the guidelines and expand or restrict the entries in the system log. As with other documentation, the rules for a system log are not etched in stone—they can and should be modified to match the current operating environment.

9.10 SUMMARY OF KEY POINTS

☐ Good internal documentation helps MIS staff members in their day-to-day and week-to-week activities by increasing productivity.

☐ Documentation can help with maintenance, explain the processing of a program and system, and serve as "requirements" for the program's eventual replacement.

☐ All internal documentation must follow the same set of standards, even if the standards are not the best.

☐ Internal documentation is cost-justified only when management takes the long-range view. Technical documentation for the staff should be looked on as a long-term business investment.

☐ A good data dictionary can link together all internal documentation and the actual source code. An active dictionary is better than a passive one.

☐ The results of every investigation that takes more than thirty minutes of actual programmer or analyst time should be documented either in a user manual, in a technical manual, or directly in the program.

☐ Automated flowchart packages are justified on the basis of increased productivity.

☐ Every application needs both an answer book and a system log. The answer book holds valuable miscellaneous information that does not fit in other documentation, and the system log lists important events in the history of that application. Both documents are valuable aids to the technical staff responsible for production support.

Appendix

Word-Processing Requirements

Since word processing is available on everything from a lap-sized microcomputer to the largest mainframe, MIS management may have a choice between two general directions with several word-processing packages in each mode. Depending on the long-term situation, management may prefer stand-alone word processors (e.g., a single-user microcomputer) or a shared word-processing system (e.g., a minicomputer) that allows many staff members to update, review, and share the same written material.

Most word-processing systems have category A requirements. Category B features are very useful when producing long documents, such as user manuals and system designs. Category C functions are nice to have, but not essential.

CATEGORY A REQUIREMENTS

- A full-screen text editor.
- The ability to copy, delete, and rearrange lines and paragraphs as needed, and the ability to selectively merge parts of other documents into a new one.
- Boldface and underlining capability.
- Automatic backup of each document before the current version is saved on disk.
- An archival feature allowing the author to save at least one past version of the document, or to backout all changes made during the current session.
- Variable tabs that can be changed for each paragraph, allowing columns and straight text to appear on the same page.
- A feature that aligns text and divides words into syllables on different lines.
- Margin alignment by paragraph.
- Automatic centering of titles.
- An online help feature keyed to specific functions.
- A command that will backout the previous command or action.
- A search and search/replace feature for words or phrases.
- A way to easily access specific pages without paging sequentially through the entire document.
- A variable line-spacing feature.
- The ability to print specific page numbers or a range of page numbers.
- A feature that will allow printing of multiple copies of the same document.

CATEGORY B REQUIREMENTS

- A dictionary feature that automatically checks spelling, and a programmable dictionary for technical words that can be updated by the author.
- An option that will generate chapter and section headings on each page, so that readers know exactly where they are at all times.
- A storage area that holds "boilerplate" formats.
- A search capability that enables authors to scan all documents and locate those with a specific keyword.

- "Description" and "comments" labels for each document, and the ability to scan the labels for all documents.
- The ability to add footnotes and headers of more than one line to a page or set of pages.
- A feature that automatically flags every line changed during an editing session or since a previous version.
- The ability to store internal notes that will not be printed but will rather serve as reminders to the author.
- A code that tells the status of the document (a "1" may mean "production version," whereas a "2" may indicate a document in the editing stage).
- The ability to copy screen formats directly from an application into a document.
- Graphics capability for the common data-processing symbols, such as squares, rectangles, and diamonds.

CATEGORY C REQUIREMENTS

- A library that holds commonly used words, phrases, and paragraphs, with the capability to insert them into a document with a single command.
- Indexing features that allow automatic cross-reference for author-selected keywords.
- The choice of 80 or 132 print positions, and a CRT that supports both formats without horizontal scrolling.
- A multiprocessing feature that allows the author to edit one document while printing another.
- Different type fonts selected at each printing session.
- A readability index that gives a computed "difficulty" level for each paragraph in a document.
- A way to view documents on the CRT exactly as they will be printed.
- Multiple windows that allow the author to view more than one document at a time (helpful for comparing two or more user manuals).
- A "password protection" feature for sensitive documents.

Indexes

247

FORMS INDEX